AF887257

Daughter

Tae,

I love and adore you lil sis!

Love forever,

Tawana B

Daughter

Created to Belong – Book 1

TAWANA DARSHAE BURKS

DAUGHTER

Created to Belong – Book 1

November Media Publishing

ISBN-13: 978-0-578-91614-9

Dedicated to

All who have dealt with childhood trauma, rejection, and abandonment. Know that you are not forgotten. You are loved with an everlasting love.

Also dedicated to all of my friends and loved ones who encouraged me and supported me throughout this journey. My dearest friend Veronica Holmes, thank you for always being there, and for helping me with this assignment. I am so blessed to have you as a friend. A special shoutout to my friend and brother Alain Joseph who made sure this assignment came forth. I could not have done it without you!

Table of Contents

CHAPTER 1

The Daughter

Karissa sat deathly still in the waiting area of Interfaith Counseling Center. Flashes of Sariah's voice echoed in her memory as she tried to trace back through her decision to come in the first place. Closing her eyes, she allowed herself to go back in time. She was sitting in Sariah's living room when Sariah seemed to pounce on her.

"Karissa, this is the fifth panic attack you've had this week. You have to seek some help."

"I just need rest. It's not that big of a deal." She tried to sound more composed than she felt. She feared she was pregnant at that point, and that added to her sense of panic. She usually tried not to share those types of things with her overly concerned friend. She did tell her she was dealing with something that involved a guy, and that's what caused her to be so anxious. While Sariah hadn't asked questions, Karissa knew she probably guessed the issue. Sariah had a way of knowing her thoughts. Steve was an OK guy, but she would never want to have a child with him. Or anyone for that matter.

Karissa sipped from her glass of cool tea to douse the fire burning inside her. She purposely ignored Sariah's piercing glare.

The flat-screen above the mantle was tuned to the animal channel. The dreary unanimated voice babbled on about the American Black Bear. Sariah rarely watched TV, but it was usually some worship music playing from YouTube when she did. Or something from the National Geographic channel. Sariah loved animals, but Karissa thought they were a disturbance to human life.

Sariah got up from the cream-colored ottoman that faced Karissa, who sat on the couch. Sariah gave an exhausted sigh as she stood and threw her hands in the air. "Fine, Karissa, it's your life. You know how I feel. I won't keep talking for the heck of it." She walked to the kitchen.

Even though Karissa was annoyed with Sariah's attempts to direct her life, she felt crappy for dumping all her issues on her friend. She had a full-blown panic attack not even fifteen minutes before walking through the door, and she knew it was not cool to blow Sariah off for trying to give her advice.

Even if the advice wasn't what she wanted to hear, she knew she should have at least listened.

Looking back over the couch, Karissa took a deep breath and released it. "Look 'Riah, thank you for always having my back. I know I busted into your place with my drama as usual. I love you, girl." She laughed lightly, trying to ease the mood.

Sariah held back tears of frustration as she poured herself a glass of tea. Karissa always said Sariah could find anything to cry about. But it touched Karissa that someone as genuine as Sariah loved her enough to display such deep emotions over her foolishness. She saw the wearied way Sariah placed the tea pitcher back into the refrigerator.

"You've known me since college Sariah, and you know I'm different than you. I can't throw myself helplessly at a God I can't see and people that bleed as I bleed. They are just as screwed up as I am. I'm not about to pay some book-learned therapist to tell me things about myself that I already know."

"God…" Sariah said as she turned to Karissa, gripping the back of her neck as her shoulders tensed.

Karissa put her head down because she knew Sariah was engaging with her God. Sariah did that often during their conversations. It no longer bothered Karissa nor made her uncomfortable. She found it amusing and wanted to laugh.

Her friend was beating a dead horse with her, but she did not want to further upset her. Karissa relented. "Fine, Sariah, I'll go to the stupid therapist, but I only promise one visit." She was annoyed when she saw Sariah with a cheerful smile on her face.

Karissa began grabbing her things. She was ready to go now that Sariah had worked her emotions enough to get what she wanted.

"Oh, Karissa, you'll love it!" Sariah exclaimed as if she was stunned at how fast her God had answered her prayers.

Karissa rolled her eyes as Sariah came and flopped on the couch next to her. Sariah wrapped her in a sisterly embrace. "Whatever, Sariah. I'm just looking forward to coming back and letting you know how much it wasted my time. Then you can pay me back all one hundred billion dollars it cost to see this therapist person."

Sariah laughed as she pulled back, still holding Karissa's shoulders as if she was a schoolgirl. "Look, Karissa, you still have to give it a chance. Don't go in there acting crazy. You have to be open. You won't come back to church with me, go to the small group with me anymore, or anything, so at least have an open mind in therapy. I have the perfect counselor for you to check out."

So, now here she was at Interfaith Counseling Center, following through on her promise. Karissa fidgeted with her watch. She knew she would regret letting Sariah convince her to make this appointment. After all, the only people that found themselves in places like this were emotionally weak. Those who had no strength or pride to figure out their issues. But she wanted to be able to tell Sariah that she at least tried.

Karissa sat in the waiting room with her floppy hat on, trying to salvage her dignity, hoping no one would notice her. She gazed at the large antique clock with Victorian-style gold trimming on the white wall in front of her. The receptionist busied herself with whatever was on her computer screen. The loud stillness of the waiting room grated on her nerves.

Just as she was about to pick her phone up to search her call log, she heard light, quick steps coming her way. She jerked her head up and saw a woman with shoulder-length blond hair walking towards her. She immediately sat up in her chair. Was this her psychologist or therapist or whatever they called themselves? She could have sworn Sariah told her it was a black woman. She gripped the arm of the chair, attempting not to curse her strong-willed friend who would have said just almost anything to get her to show up.

As the woman drew closer, she could see tears in her beautiful blue eyes. Karissa immediately felt uneasy. Why would she be crying? Who was she? Karissa pulled down the brim of her hat to block her vision.

She gave the woman a strained smile as she walked past her, heading towards the elevator less than ten feet away. The woman had completely ignored her, which she understood, considering her emotional state. That, and the fact that she probably looked like a creep smiling incognito with her eyes hidden underneath the hat.

Karissa lowered her head to ease her embarrassment at noticing the woman's frail state. Now, she saw the woman's slender frame swing around gracefully toward her as she waited for the elevator. The woman returned the act with a smile of her own, as painful as it may have been. Karissa felt strangely touched by the woman. She could almost feel her pain even though she had never seen her before. Sobs suddenly washed over the woman.

"I'm sorry, Mrs. Winston. Would you like to set up your next appointment?" The soft but rushed voice came from the receptionist who had just looked up from her work and noticed the woman.

The elevator bell rang, signaling its arrival. Mrs. Winston stuck her foot in to stop the doors from closing. "No thank you, Ramona. I'll call with my next available time. Thank you, dear." With that, she was on the elevator, weeping into her palms as the doors closed.

Karissa looked over at Ramona, who began to focus again, with tight lips and a determined look, on the task before her. Karissa gazed away, took in a deep breath, and exhaled slowly.

Karissa's mind began to stray into realms of self-doubt. What was she thinking by coming here in the first place? She shook her head slightly as if she was shaking herself out of a trance. She quickly grabbed her cross-body bag that was hanging on the back of the chair. She was going to leave this place before the receptionist could protest her decision.

Just as she started for the elevator, she heard one of the most calming voices she had ever heard. "Ms. Sparks, thank you for your patience. I'm sorry your wait was longer than usual. Please follow me." A woman was standing near the receptionist's desk. She had smooth brown skin, big beautiful eyes, and a ponytail with the most perfectly round bun she had ever seen.

The receptionist handed the woman a yellow file folder. Karissa felt chills up her spine, and the hairs stand up on her arms. She couldn't run at this point.

Karissa paused to consider her options. She could pretend that she had another appointment. Still, she had already told the receptionist that she cleared her schedule for the day. Or she could pretend that she was not feeling well. But that would look like a cop-out because she did not look ill.

The therapist held out her hand the way a schoolteacher would, motioning Karissa to follow her. Karissa walked towards a session she was sure would be a waste of time and money.

Dr. Phillips was her name, according to Sariah. She had raved about her for years, but that had gone in one ear and out the other. Karissa vowed several times that she would never waste her money this way, and now she felt like she was being led like a lamb to the slaughter.

Nevertheless, Karissa wanted to be polite. "Hello, I am Karissa Sparks. It's a pleasure to meet you." She held out her hand.

"Hello, Ms. Sparks. It's a pleasure to meet you finally. I'm Dr. Phillips"—as she reached her hand out and took Karissa's in hers. Karissa's body warmed at the magnetic smile and touch. Lifting her hat just a little, Karissa noticed Dr. Phillips' easy sincerity, and the tension in her neck eased.

As they walked together down the hall, Karissa started to admire the Interfaith Counseling Center offices' grandeur. They filled the entire sixth floor. They walked a little further down the hallway, past the restrooms, a lunch area, and a couple more personal offices, and finally walked into Dr. Phillip's office.

Karissa quivered mildly when she stepped into the office. It was a simple, elegant room, but she felt something when she walked through the doors. It was larger than she expected, about two hundred square feet, she guessed, with all off-white walls. The floors were a striking chestnut wood with a blue plush rug covering a large portion of the office. Tropical Dracaena plants reached far and wide from either side of the office—it reminded her of one of her Pinterest boards. There was a drink bar immediately to the left of the door with water, tea, and soft drinks.

There was a comfortable-looking black leather recliner. It was extended to what seemed to be her exact height of five feet seven inches, and it beckoned her to lay down on it. She eyed it cautiously. It was similar to the ones she saw in those emotional movies where someone has to visit a therapist. She mocked it in her thoughts. *Oh, how she had judged and inwardly cringed at the characters in those movies, and look at her now, she thought.* She scolded herself for her hypocrisy.

She noticed a small glass desk with a chair behind it, obviously where Dr. Phillips sat. The office had minimal decorations on the walls, but it didn't need much as the off-white shouted loud enough. It made Karissa feel like she was suspended in time and floating on clouds. The peace of the office serenaded tranquility and took the edge off Karissa's anxiety and fear. The air smelled of warm vanilla. The fragrance emanated from a candle on the bookshelf adjacent to Dr. Phillips's desk.

As she continued to survey the office, she noticed awards on the wall recognizing "Dr. Amanda Phillips." One was from the Foster Care Movement of New York. Her thoughts quickened as she tried to calculate the irony. This had to be one of the reasons Sariah was adamant about her seeing Dr. Phillips.

"Ms. Sparks, please feel free to have a seat if you'd like." Dr. Philips said, interrupting the whirlwind of thoughts swirling in her mind.

Suddenly, Karissa's head began to throb, and she found it hard to breathe. She turned her back, determined not to have a full-blown panic attack in front of this woman.

Breathe Karissa, Breathe, in and out, in and out....

"Karissa, are you OK?" Dr. Phillips asked, concerned.

"I'm... I'm fine." she stuttered. She turned around and forced a smile as she felt the thumps of her heart slowing. Karissa sat down, trying to still her shaking body. She decided that she would not lay down as if she was some helpless person. Instead, she adjusted the recliner to an upright position.

With the smooth leatherlike chair comforting her, Karissa started thinking of some rules of engagement. She preferred not to be called "Ms. Sparks." It reminded her of her single status that she often tried to ignore. She would politely suggest to Dr. Phillips to refer to her as Karissa.

"Ms. Sparks, what...." Before Dr. Phillips could get the question out, Karissa interjected, "Please call me Karissa."

She noticed that Dr. Philips's face remained soft and gentle, and she continued to smile at her. "Okay, Karissa. What brings you in today?"

This was the million-dollar question, Karissa thought to herself. She didn't answer right away.

She had filled out an in-take form before her visit. She was unable to identify a need then either. She took a deep breath, wondering how to answer Dr. Phillips' question. She knew this question would eventually have to be answered, and she rehearsed all the things she would say when asked.

The sweet smell of the room intoxicated her and almost distracted her from the question at hand. She inhaled the vanilla scent. She relaxed and sank deeply into the chair and opened her mouth for the first time in what seemed like an eternity.

With pursed lips, she clasped her hands together before responding. "The thing is that I wouldn't say that I have a 'need,'" she emphasized as she crossed her legs apprehensively. "My friend Sariah suggested that I come." She cleared her throat. "Well, because a lot of our friends have seen counselors for various reasons and swear that it's been great for their mental and emotional health." She paused and swallowed the lump in her throat.

"I have had some challenges, but I'm sure it's nothing outside the scope of what's normal" she shrugged.

Karissa could feel the erratic pounding in her chest and couldn't understand why she was so nervous.

She took a deep breath and said, "So, to answer your question, Dr. Philips—to be honest, I don't really know why I'm here."

Dr. Philips looked through the papers attached to her clipboard, a confused look on her face. She stopped on a page and looked up at Karissa. She let out an unintentional chuckle as she let the pages fall back into their place.

She looked Karissa in the eye. “Well, you mentioned that you have been having nearly debilitating panic attacks, nightmares, and thoughts that keep you distracted from your work. Are you still struggling with these things?” Dr. Phillips asked.

“Um, yeah, I guess you can say that would be reason enough to see a therapist,” she said with forced restraint.

“Look, Karissa, I would love to help you if you allow me, but I need for us to work together. From what you have identified on your intake form, I believe that we can get to the bottom of your attacks, but I need you to trust the process. Be willing to take the journey with me.” Dr. Phillips put her forearms on the desk and rested her chin on her hands, a pensive look on her face. Her words were kind but direct.

Karissa hadn’t expected to do any work or go through any processes. She expected to be asked some basic questions about her childhood, given some advice, and sent on her way. She had expected to go back to Sariah and let her know that she would have to pay for it the next time she wanted to fix her life. But she didn’t want anyone peering over the wall she had so carefully constructed to protect herself.

Yes, there had been times she tried to unleash all of her confused thoughts and emotions on people. But they only pitied her, looked down on her, or suggest she talk with a professional. She despised it all. Yet, Karissa knew there was a yearning within that she had not been able to resolve by herself.

CHAPTER 2

Amanda's Perspective

Dr. Amanda Phillips sank deep into her chair as she awaited her next appointment with a young woman named Karissa. She pressed her hands firmly together across her lap. *"Lord, I am not going after Mrs. Winston this time unless you lead me to do it. I don't know what to say to her when she gets like this. I have said everything that's in the books to say. I have even said the things I believe you have led me to say, but what good has it done?"*

She heard no response as she leaned her head back against the coolness of the leather chair. It brought a euphoric sensation that eased her thoughts. This silent, empty space was so full of the ever-embracing presence of God. The bright light beaming through the wall-to-wall window reminded her it was not time to rest. She loved sitting there, allowing the silence to still her before her next session—which was within the next fifteen minutes. Slowly opening her eyes, she sat there motionless, gazing out the window.

Her next client was recommended by a former client turned little sister and friend, Sariah. She had given a little background on Karissa, but not much as she didn't want to betray her friend's trust. Amanda sighed, and that released the heaviness that weighed on her heart.

Stopping just before she reached her office door, she decided to take a little longer to pray to dissipate the heaviness weighing in around her. Yes, she just needed five more minutes to pray. She walked back to her desk and sat down with new resolve. She pulled her Bible from the drawer. It was the Bible that her grandmother gave her years ago and that she kept close. It was special to her. She allowed her fingers to run over the worn leather. Smiling to herself she closed her eyes and thanked God for His peace. She flipped through the pages trying to hold some of them together as its frailty threatened to give way.

Turning to her favorite scripture, Proverbs 3:5, she allowed the words to fill her mind, pouring into her heart, then opening her mouth, she read, "Trust in the Lord with all your heart, lean not on your own understanding. Acknowledge Him in all your ways, and He will direct your path." Lightness filled her, and she swelled with assurance. She bowed her head and prayed.

"Heavenly Father, I turn my attention to you. I cast my cares unto you because I know you care for me. Release your peace like never before over me, Lord; I pray that your presence

will be tangible in this office. Bless Mrs. Winston today, and grant her peace. And bless Ms. Sparks during our session. Have your way in me, in Jesus' name, amen."

Looking at her watch, she realized she had less than ten minutes before her next client. She decided to see if Ramona spoke with Mrs. Winston.

As Amanda approached Ramona, a bustling sound caught her attention. She glanced over and noticed a young woman gathering her things as if she was getting ready to leave. "Ms. Sparks?" Amanda asked. Karissa looked up, and Amanda could see the coming journey through the frightened eyes staring back at her.

Back in her office, Amanda sat down in her chair directly across from the client's recliner. "Ms. Sparks, please feel free to have a seat if you'd like." She smiled warmly at Karissa. She couldn't help but notice how beautiful the young woman was. She was in her mid-twenties, judging by her youthful face and outfit—which spoke of professionalism with a hint of edginess. She had on an oversized floppy hat as if she didn't want to be recognized. Rebellious curls spilled from the sides of her hat, exposing beautiful curly brown hair. Her caramel skin looked as if she had never struggled with defiant breakouts. Her smile made the room a little lighter, although the young woman had a mysterious sadness. Her physical build was one that Amanda had worked out three times a week to obtain and still fell short in achieving.

Amanda noticed in the moment that she greeted her in the waiting area that the young woman was embarrassed to be there. She could tell that Karissa was proud, and may resist the faith component of her counseling approach. But she promised herself that she would not judge. If God led Karissa into her office, then she would allow Him to do exactly what He intended to do.

Amanda noticed Karissa glancing at an award on her wall. She wondered what caused the young woman to be so enraptured by it. Amanda had been a therapist for close to fifteen years. She had practiced in New York for the past five years and was heavily involved in the foster care system.

"That's the one accolade I'm proud to display," Amanda said, smiling brightly. "I have a heart for the youth in foster care and those who have been adopted," she said, pulling in a deep breath. Amanda's eyes went into a distant look as if she was envisioning it all. Warily drawing her attention back to the present, Amanda sank a little deeper in her chair and sat back in an unhurried manner.

She noted that her comments made Karissa uncomfortable and wondered why. "Please feel free to have a seat," as she pointed to the chair. Karissa returned a forced smile as she walked back straight, head high towards the chair. Amanda noticed Karissa might have wanted to respond to her comment. Still, her stern face let Amanda know she wasn't ready to open up. Karissa adjusted the recliner and sat down.

Amanda chided herself for neglecting to reposition the chair from its reclining position after Mrs. Winston's session.

Amanda noticed the contrived smile Karissa attempted to give. "Ms. Sparks, what…" "Please call me Karissa," Karissa interjected matter-of-factly.

"OK, Karissa. What brings you in today?" Amanda allowed the question to linger in the air comfortably as she watched Karissa deliberate about how to respond. She learned throughout her career not to be uncomfortable with silence. Never rush the conversation. Always go at the client's pace.

"The thing is that I wouldn't say that I have a 'need'. My friend Sariah suggested that I come. Well, because a lot of our friends have seen counselors for various reasons, and swear that it's been great for their "mental and emotional health." Karissa used her fingers to mock the quotation. "I have had some challenges, but I'm sure it's nothing outside the scope of what's normal."

Amanda observed that Karissa was trying to convince herself that she was telling the truth. She also smiled at the mention of sweet, energetic, and zealous Sariah. She loved Sariah and the influence that she had on her own life throughout their journey together.

Sariah had come in for sessions last year and had recently stopped attending. Their sessions had become less of Amanda helping Sariah and more of girlfriends encouraging one another in the Lord. Amanda had suggested that Sariah stop paying for sessions, as she felt Sariah encouraged her most of the time. Sariah refused. Amanda was convinced that the Lord sent Sariah to her to help her remain sane in her career, or "calling," as she liked to put it.

"So, to answer your question, Dr. Phillips—I don't really know why I'm here."

Amanda gave Karissa a warm smile to settle her nerves. Karissa looked as if she had stubborn tears refusing to leave the safety of her deep brown eyes. She blinked the tears away, immediately sucked in some air, and exhaled.

"So, where do we start?" Karissa asked as if she was expecting to hear, "Thank you for the visit, but since you are perfectly fine, you don't seem to need a therapist after all."

But instead, Amanda started with, "Tell me about Karissa Sparks. Wherever you want to start."

CHAPTER 3

The Dream

As Karissa walked the busy Manhattan streets headed to the subway and her cozy apartment in Brooklyn, she couldn't help but feel lighter. There was something eerily strange and freeing about her session with Dr. Phillips.

Was it the quaintness of her East Houston Street office? Or maybe it was the way she could share things with a stranger with an unbiased opinion. Whatever it was, it wasn't bad after all. She shuddered at the prospect of having to say it to her face, but maybe Sariah was right.

Dr. Phillips didn't get too far into her past, and she was grateful for that. She wasn't sure she was ready to dive into such a vulnerable part of her life yet. After all, there were things she hadn't even pondered or addressed within herself. She wasn't ready to open up about those things with a stranger, paid or not.

She thought about her conversation with Dr. Phillips as she walked. They talked about Karissa's life after she moved to New York two years ago from North Carolina. She had landed her then dream job—as a marketing strategist with Push Marketing, Inc. in Midtown Manhattan.

She had studied Marketing at Brookdale University in Charlotte, North Carolina. She was excited about a change of pace in life. She was good at what she did but knew she still had a great deal to learn. Joining one of the top marketing firms with no real experience came with its challenges. She shared some of those challenges with Dr. Phillips—how she felt the need to prove herself constantly. She also shared about her social life, her friends, and what she enjoyed doing for fun.

Karissa was good at making friends and felt connected with a lot of people. However, she did not let many of them into her world. She was vulnerable with no one and could not recall a time where she cried on someone's shoulder. She often offered her shoulder to others but did not allow others to enter her emotionally vulnerable world. She was closest to Sariah, who knew most of her past and many of her insecurities and fears. Dr. Phillips hadn't seemed turned off or bothered by anything Karissa shared, and that allowed her to relax.

She was almost to the subway when she escaped her thoughts and realized it was a beautiful sunny day, although it was only sixty-nine degrees. The wind bumped up against her face chaotically, causing her to grab her hat, holding it in place. She loved days like this. She smiled to herself as stone-faced New Yorkers rushed in all directions, each absorbed in their own world.

In Karissa's talk with Dr. Phillips, she became more open to the idea of exploring why she was so guarded. She wanted to be as free as Sariah, but not at the expense of blindly following a God she couldn't even see.

* * *

When Karissa finally made it back to her apartment, she threw her jacket and bag on the coat rack, walked across the room, and flung herself on her cozy couch she loved so much. Yes, it was only 6:30 PM, but she was exhausted. She would rest for about an hour before she had to get up and get ready. She promised Rachel that she would go to a co-worker's birthday party a couple of weeks ago. It was Friday, and she was grateful for a couple of days off from a demanding schedule at work.

She reached for one of the plush pillows, grabbed her white fur blanket from behind the couch, and made herself comfortable. She felt her eyes getting heavier and tried to note her weekend plans mentally. She was fast asleep before she made it to Saturday's schedule.

She fell into a dark, terrifying hole in her dream.

All Karissa could hear was the deafening screams in her ears as she raced through the familiar home towards the para-

lyzing cries coming from upstairs. Heart pounding in her chest as she bent the corner at what felt like full speed. "Hold on, here I come, please...." she managed to muffle out in short gasps while she tried to catch her breath.

The cries were coming from what she was sure was a little girl. Karissa had no children, but the cries pierced her heart as if she was intimately connected to the tormented child. She turned the corner exiting living room, running down the hallway that seemed to have no end, and noticed a faded wooden door on the left that led upstairs. The house was not large, but it was long and had many twists and turns.

She slowed down enough to reach for the door as she gasped for air. She heard another scream that broke through her exhaustion. Opening the door, Karissa looked up the stairs and could not believe it. The stairs were countless, and she couldn't see where they led. Nevertheless, she took them on two at a time, running as if her life depended on it—trying to reach the child.

Dizziness closed in around her after making it past what felt like dozens of stairs. Her eyes were heavy with exhaustion. Slowing down, she heard a piercing doorbell ringing in her ears. Before she knew it, she began to fall backwards down the stairs that she had conquered—her body almost weightless against gravity. She tried to grab hold of the handrail plastered on the faded yellow wall, but her hand slipped through the rail as if it was only there in her imagination.

Before she could feel the impact of the fall, she woke up—heart beating wildly in a manner that felt as if it would burst through her chest.

Sweat and perspiration beaded on her forehead. Alarm going off, Karissa shook her head frantically, reaching over mindlessly for her phone to silence the alarm. Foggy-minded, she was unsure if it was just a dream. She placed her phone back on the coffee table and began to cry. Her face lay helplessly in the palm of her hands as she wept. Her body shook with every sob reminding her that she was alive, awake, that she existed.

She rehearsed the dream with every draining sob. She felt like she was in a trance. She reached for a box of tissues on the stand next to her couch and wiped her tears.

This was not the first dream she had with the screaming child. She didn't understand why these dreams persisted or why she reacted so grievously each time. But she did know one thing: she did not have time to ponder it too much. She would do with this dream what she did with her past—discard it altogether and move on. She had better things to do, and she couldn't allow herself to spiral into an emotional frenzy.

Karissa was a frequent dreamer. She had emotionally daunting dreams since she was a child. Some of her dreams foretold of things that happened. Some revealed things about where she was emotionally, and others, well, she couldn't quite figure out their purpose.

Sariah sometimes taught her about how God speaks to people in dreams and visions. But Karissa was not entirely convinced that God was as intimately involved with the daily affairs of humans. She would often find herself combating the naïve faith of Sariah and others. "How could you say God is involved when there are homeless people, racism, murders, and unfair things that happen to innocent people all the time?"

No, Karissa would not be taken in by the blind faith embraced by people like Sariah. Karissa was not altogether convinced that God was real. She had moments where she could feel things that she couldn't describe in words, but that didn't mean anything. For example, whenever she went to church with Sariah, which was no more than a dozen times since she had known her, she would often sense someone touching her shoulder. It was weird and would freak her out as she found herself looking over her shoulder at times, asking if someone touched her. But Karissa had been through enough in her life to know that God was not involved in the mundane lives of ordinary people.

Karissa jumped franticly as she heard the ring of her cellphone. She was annoyed by the disruption. She picked it up, ready to send whoever was on the other end straight to voicemail.

As she drew the phone closer, she saw Rachel's name sliding across the screen. She looked at the time, and it read 7:30 PM. Her heart seemed to sink into her stomach, remembering the plans they had for the evening.

"Rachel! I'm so sorry. I'm just seeing the time. I fell asleep when I got home today and lost track of time."

"It's fine, girl. The party doesn't start till 8 PM, so we can make it across the Manhattan Bridge and get into town in plenty of time. How long will it take you to get ready? I'll be there in twenty minutes."

Karissa's mind began to race, wondering if she should just cancel her plans or if she felt like dealing with the backlash that would come if she did. This would be her third time canceling plans with Rachel this month, so she decided against it. She swung her legs off the couch and proceeded to propel herself up before responding to Rachel. She felt lightheaded and had to reach for the arm of the couch for balance. Once steady on her feet, she walked zombie-like to her bedroom.

"Karissa, you there?" Rachel asked.

"Yes," Karissa responded, "I'm here."

Karissa began peeling off her clothes in her bedroom, wondering what she was going to wear. "I should be ready when you get here. What are you wearing?" she asked. She was still distant and in a haze from the dream.

"I'm wearing my black cocktail dress—the one I wore at Andrew's birthday party last month. It's the one that is tight at the top and flairs out above the knees."

Rachel looked great in that dress, Karissa remembered. She sorted through the dress section of her walk-in closet, looking for something that wouldn't make her look like she was begging for attention. She loved to show up and show out when she went out, but this was just a party for one of Rachel's co-workers. She wasn't in the mood to do too much. Besides, Rachel had been trying to hook her up lately. She didn't want to give her friend any ammunition to try harder.

"Yes, I love that dress," Karissa said. She tried to sound enthusiastic about the night, although what she wanted to do was lay back down and sleep.

"Karissa, promise me that you won't come out looking like you are trying to scare off men. I know you are not interested in being hooked up, so please don't try to prove a point and come out looking lame."

Karissa laughed. She knew Rachel was not trying to be mean. Rachel knew her well enough to know what she was thinking.

"Whatever, Rachel. I know how to dress for the occasion. Besides, I'm not thinking about that." She began to shift her attention to the red dress in her closet. It fit her body perfectly and hugged her curves better than other choices she could have made.

"Yeah, OK," Rachel retorted with a less than halfhearted laugh.

"Ok, I think I know what I'm going to wear. I'll see you when you get here," Karissa said hurriedly, hanging up the phone and tossing it on her bed.

It had been a while since she went out; she could use a quick pick-me-up. Glancing in her floor-length mirror next to her closet, Karissa's eyes bulged at the sight of herself. Her hair was a plastered messily in a sloppy bun at the top of her head. Dark paths of eyeliner coursed her cheeks from the tears she had cried. Yes, she thought to herself. A pick-me-up will do the trick.

Rachel was wrong about one thing—it wasn't that Karissa didn't want to be with someone. Of course, she wanted love. She wanted to be loved by someone unconditionally after they knew everything about her. She had always struggled in that area and felt that it was all too complicated. She decided to just use men for what she needed, enjoy the brief encounters, but never let things go too far.

Karissa wanted many things, but just because she wanted them didn't mean she would get them. There was a gaping hole somewhere inside her, and she was too afraid she would dissolve into madness someday. She didn't want the complications love would bring when that happened. She had given her heart away once and was left devastated. She vowed she wouldn't do it again.

CHAPTER 4

The Party

Karissa ran to the door when she heard someone banging on it to a beat. She knew Rachel had arrived.

Rachel gasped, placing her hand to her mouth in a playful shocked manner. "Karissa, honey, you look stunning! Are you trying to give every man there a heart attack?"

She had decided to wear one of her favorites— a cobalt blue dress that hung off the shoulders. She contrasted it with matte red pumps and wore her hair in her natural curls, which hung past her shoulders. She did not want to overdo it, so she kept her make-up tastefully simple.

Karissa laughed and embraced her friend. She loved Rachel. They had met almost two years ago at the Push Marketing's Christmas party, and discovered they lived near each other in Brooklyn. Rachel was the niece of the former director of P.R., and her aunt adored her. Rachel was a bit loud and had no filter whatsoever. Karissa loved that about her. She never had to guess what Rachel thought, which made it easier to trust her. If it came to her mind, Rachel spoke it. She always had good intentions, but you could sometimes be offended by her bluntness if you did not know her well. She would hug everyone and made no one feel like an outsider. Rachel was the youngest of three children and the only girl.

Rachel was not a Christian, and Karissa liked that about her too. She was not preachy like Sariah. Rachel was one of those people who took life as it came. She was a free spirit who didn't take herself too seriously. However, free-spirited Rachel was a successful young woman. She received her master's degree in engineering at NYU, and she made more money than a lot of people twice her age. At twenty-seven years old, she was doing well for herself.

Rachel had the physical build of an athlete. She often complained about her body, especially when she was in the range of Karissa's glow. She said her breasts looked like her three-year-old niece's or that her legs made her look like she was on steroids. She was unaware that Karissa was secretly envious of Rachel's smooth chocolate skin and dreamy eyes.

"How long will you be," Rachel asked as she sauntered to the couch and plopped down.

"Just need to grab my purse. Are you going to drive?" Karissa asked as she hurried to her bedroom. She hated driving in the city and avoided it as much as she could.

"Yes," Rachel said sarcastically, rolling her eyes. "I'll drive. You know you aren't going to take your SUV out of that privileged parking spot. By the way, when is Kent coming back from his assignment in Africa?"

Karissa could hear the mocking edge in her friend's voice. She laughed before she spoke. "I would if you don't want to deal with the traffic. It's not that far anyway," she said, coming out, placing the strap of her bag over her shoulder. "And Kent? He'll be away for about six more months, so I'll enjoy that free protected parking spot for a while."

"I'll drive," Rachel said. "You know things would have gotten awkward if I said you should drive, and you know it." She laughed as she grabbed a bottle of water from the counter.

"True." Karissa giggled as she slipped into her heels. "OK, come on brat." Rachel flipped Karissa's hair as she headed to the door.

Karissa was relieved that Rachel decided to drive. She was still drowsy from the nap she took and was not up to driving around trying to find parking. It was a chilly fall night in New York City. Manhattan was filled with all kinds of people as usual. At Fourteenth Street and Park Avenue, Karissa noticed about thirty Asians rushing out of tour buses. She saw a group of teenagers dressed like they were going to a party but didn't seem old enough to get into it. Other people darted quickly in all directions. She loved to watch as people lived their lives, wondering about the stories of each one.

"So, how was your visit with the psych chick?" Rachel asked, forcing Karissa to take a deep breath and refocus her attention.

Karissa paused to give thought to the question before answering.

"What the heck is wrong with you!?" Rachel shouted, slamming on her brakes abruptly as a lane-switching taxicab cut them off, almost causing an accident. This is the one thing you get when you ride with Rachel, Karissa thought to herself. The girl has severe road rage.

"Rachel, breathe girl."

Rachel rolled her eyes, more at the situation than Karissa. "You were saying?" Rachel asked, trying to sound more in control of her emotions. Karissa looked around to see how close they were to their destination, more out of anxiety than curiosity. They still had another fifteen minutes, according to the flow of traffic and Rachel's GPS.

"It wasn't bad at all," Karissa finally said. "I was definitely about to run out of the office before she even called me back. But I'm glad I didn't leave. I still think it's a bit useless and weird, but I'm interested to an extent. So, I'm going back for another session."

Karissa smiled to herself, thinking about how smooth her conversation went with Dr. Phillips. They hadn't got involved in a deep conversation, but she felt willing to go back.

That had to mean something considering it took Sariah years of convincing her before she decided to go.

"Well, that's a shock coming from you, Ms. 'I'll never give my money to someone to tell me the same thing I can figure out on Google,'" Rachel said, mocking Karissa.

"Why do you remember every conversation?" Karissa asked with a smile on her lips. She wondered how Rachel was always able to remind her of something silly she said in the past.

"Well, Karissa, because they're so entertaining," she said, laughing out loud. She glanced over at Rachel as she shook her head, a grin on her face.

"I'm not sure what I'm looking for, or even why I'm seeing a therapist for that matter." Karissa turned back to people-watching, allowing her words to roll over in her mind. The fogginess of her breath against the passenger window was an outward expression of the haze she felt in her mind. Pulling her face away from the window, she answered, "I mean, yes, the nightmares and panic attacks haven't stopped, but they haven't been as bad as they used to be." She breathed deeply and released the tension. She closed her eyes, pulling air into her lungs and forcing it out. She just wanted to ride in peace. Not be hounded by questions.

"Are you afraid of what might come up in your sessions with her? Are you ready to dig up things from your past that you don't even like to deal with yourself?" Rachel turned the corner sharply, and Karissa's body jerked in the opposite direction. "My bad girl. Almost missed my turn."

Looking at Rachel, Karissa pondered if she wanted to tell her to leave well enough alone or answer her question. She could see the worried way Rachel bit her lip and knew her friend felt uneasy about asking. Rachel, like Sariah, knew how much Karissa was usually willing to disclose.

Karissa sighed, "I don't know. Maybe. I honestly haven't looked that far down the road. I wouldn't mind understanding why I keep having these dreams and panic attacks."

"You think she will be able to help you figure that out? What happened to Sariah's church friend?"

"She helped a little with understanding dreams and stuff, but I didn't want to deal with someone who was pushing their beliefs on me."

"Well, if that were the case, you wouldn't deal with Sariah, 'cause Lord knows she has no chill."

"That's true, but Sariah is like family. It's a little different with her. She's not going anywhere even if I tried to make her go. The girl is stuck like glue."

"And you love it," Rachel said with a slight edge.

"Yeah, I guess I do," Karissa responded without taking offense. She knew Rachel and Sariah didn't see eye-to-eye, but she knew they both loved her—just maybe in different ways.

"Sariah does too much sometimes," Rachel said. "I love that girl, but I honestly think she comes on too strong. I think there is room for therapists or whatnot, but it sounds like she implied you're too broken to figure life out on your own. She's just too by-the-book for me."

Rachel paused to breathe, shrugging her shoulders slightly. She slowed down, looking to the right at the buildings they passed. "I mean, I'm glad that you went to a psychologist, but why did Sariah send you to a Christian psychologist? Was that really necessary?" Rachel was obviously annoyed with the situation.

Rachel and Sariah met at Karissa's birthday dinner a year ago. Rachel talked like this about Sariah ever since, but it didn't bother Karissa. She knew deep down Rachel respected Sariah as much as she did. She also knew that Rachel had been struggling with what to believe when it came to religion. Rachel was a self-proclaimed atheist. She came up in a Christian household but dealt with a lot of abuse as a child. She often shared how her uncle sometimes touched her inappropriately and how much of a coward her mother was for not speaking up to stop it.

Karissa shuddered at the thought of some accounts Rachel shared with her about when she was a little girl. Her uncle would call the games "hide and seek" and "pony ride"—only Rachel had no choice about playing the games. She could remember the tormented look in Rachel's eyes when Rachel first recounted these memories to her.

Her father was a workaholic who was never present emotionally. Rachel despised the Christian faith because she said it turned people into weak cowards.

"I have another appointment on Monday. We'll see where it goes. I'm not sure what I'm looking to get out of it. I guess I'll have to put some more thought into it."

Rachel hit a quick left and turned into a parking lot. "How much?" Rachel asked a short chubby guy who quickly approached the car with tickets in his hand.

"For you, twenty dollars," he said, giving a seductive glance in Karissa's direction.

Karissa rolled her eyes, unfazed at his shameless flirting.

Rachel reached into her glove compartment and pulled out a twenty-dollar bill. She pulled into the nearest parking spot.

Karissa was already tired but would not let Rachel know. She knew that her friend would get annoyed and say, "We're still young and need to act like it."

Karissa tried to change the subject, hoping it would put her in a better mood. "Anyhoo, what happened with that position you were considering? That contract that could potentially allow you to move to Cali?"

Rachel threw the gear into park and pulled her mirror down to check her lipstick. "I haven't heard back from them yet, but I'm going to send a follow-up email on Monday." She flopped the mirror back up and reached back for her purse. "I'm not pressed either way, but I wouldn't mind living my best life in Cali," she smiled mischievously.

Karissa knew if Rachel did move to California, she would fit right in with the lavish lifestyle typically associated with Hollywood. She wanted what was best for Rachel but would miss her terribly if she moved.

As they walked the block or so to the Marriott Gardens Hotel lounge, Rachel picked up the previous conversation without missing a beat. "Did you talk about your family at all?" It was clear she wanted to know more about Karissa's therapy session.

Karissa fidgeted with her purse, a bit uncomfortable with the directness of Rachel's question. A crowd of people pushed past them as if they were walking too slow. They nearly caused Karissa to trip over the trash bags lying on the sidewalk. Rachel grabbed her arm.

"'Excuse me' would work," Rachel called out at the group of men and women that had to be around their age.

One of the attractive, brown-skinned girls turned back. "Our bad, but next time try getting over to the side if you're going to walk like you have nowhere to go," she retorted in a belligerent tone.

Karissa saw fire in Rachel's eyes as she opened her mouth to fire back. Karissa knew that would get them into a fight. She grabbed Rachel's arm hard, yanking her back before she launched at the girl. "Rachel, chill. It's not that serious," Karissa exclaimed, dismissively waving her hand at the group that had stopped to back up their friend. The group turned away, muttering in low tones to each other and swearing loudly.

Rachel fought her instinct to go after the girl. "That's why I can't deal with the people in this city," Rachel said in a tone that was drenched in anger.

"You just can't let people get to you like that, Rachel," Karissa said, still on edge herself. They had to walk one behind the other so they wouldn't get bumped again. Rachel had always had a temper, but Karissa wondered why she was so quick to pounce lately.

Straightening her dress, Rachel looked at Karissa, clearly trying to compose herself. "Anyway, continue. You were answering my question seeing if you spoke about your family to the therapist lady."

Karissa was guarded about her past and her family. She never talked about it or them. Whenever asked why she never mentioned her family, she would shoot back— "Because there is nothing to talk about." Her friends would get hurt at her response, so they rarely asked her anymore.

"No, I didn't. And I'm glad that she chose not to ask me about them either."

"Well, you should be prepared to spill your guts about them if you're going to be seeing the therapist lady regularly." Rachel looked like she wanted to continue but decided against it.

Karissa thought about what Rachel said, but only for a second. She did not want Rachel formulating her own ideas of why she chose silence. "I don't have a fear of sharing. I just don't like to talk about things just for the sake of it. I have moved on, and I am living my life. I don't want anyone trying to pull me back to a place I'm no longer in."

Karissa felt herself becoming agitated. She knew that Rachel meant no harm, but that didn't mean she liked the conversation. Rachel and Sariah both had tried to get Karissa to open up about her past many times. Karissa would either change the subject or answer very dryly with comments like, "My family is doing well, I'm sure." Or "No, I'm not going home for the holidays." Or something snappy like, "Yes, I have a mother. Sure, I have a father; it takes both to bring a child into the world."

Her friends learned early that they would have to take Karissa for who she was today. However, Sariah and Rachel never relented. She knew they loved her too much to accept the level of access she was comfortable with giving them. They never went too far, but they would always ask questions in the attempt of getting her to be "in tune with her whole self." Mostly it was Sariah who did the prying.

"Fine, Karissa. I'll drop it."

"Good," Karissa responded more aggressively than she meant to sound.

* * *

When Karissa and Rachel walked into the party, the smell of expensive perfumes and musk filled the air. There had to be at least a hundred and fifty people present of different nationalities, but mostly beautiful shades of brown, which represented about sixty percent of the people present, Karissa thought. The décor was stunning. The walls were paneled in a dark wood, there were mirrors and crystal sconces, and shimmering chandeliers hung from the ceiling. She knew that whoever this co-worker was, he had money. There was a bar with beautiful women surrounding it, both sitting and standing. Men were swooning over them, trying to impress them with their smooth words and charming smiles.

Rachel spotted her co-worker, waved eagerly, and grabbed Karissa's arm, gently pulling her along before releasing her.

Karissa was overwhelmed with the scene as she hadn't expected it to be so upscale. She was glad she decided to go with the dress she had chosen.

Smooth sounds of jazz serenaded the crowd as they made their way through. She noticed the attractiveness of everyone there. Women with expensive bags and shoes, and men with tailored suits and expensive watches. She was filled with curiosity and wonder as she absorbed everything.

The moment Karissa spotted him, she froze in her tracks. She blinked twice to make sure she saw correctly.

This could not be who she thought it was. She blinked again in disbelief as they got closer, and she immediately felt her knees weaken. If it wasn't for the young lady who bumped her while trying to get past, she was sure she would have fallen into oblivion and passed out right then and there. The force of the bump snapped her back into reality. Rachel had already gone ahead.

"I'm so sorry, are you OK?" the young blond asked nervously. "Uh, yes, I'm fine," Karissa said, distracted. Karissa helped the woman pick up the things that fell from her purse. She tried to take her time focusing on the young lady, hoping that she could avoid following Rachel over to the person of the hour.

When the young woman finally walked away, Karissa had no choice but to turn around and face whatever lay before her.

She glanced over her shoulder and saw Rachel caught up in whatever she was saying. Her hands were flailing as she spoke. But all Karissa could notice was the way her heart fell into the pit of her stomach as she caught his eyes staring straight at her. She was frozen in time. She couldn't move if she tried. Her feet felt like sandbags on the marbled floor. She didn't blink, didn't swallow. She stood there motionless, like a deer caught in headlights. Everyone in the room seemed to disappear, and it was just the two of them in the ballroom of the Marriott Gardens Hotel—her and the guy she fell in love with before she moved to New York City. It dawned on her at that moment that this was indeed the birth date of Nathaniel Rye.

She saw Rachel look back, trying to see who had caught his attention in the crowd. When she saw Karissa, she looked from Nathaniel to her, then back to Nathaniel again. She motioned for Karissa to come, and Karissa blinked and walked zombie-like towards them.

"Karissa, where were you?" She didn't give her a chance to answer. "Karissa, this is Nate. Nate this is my good friend Karissa." Rachel continued as if she was unaware of the intensity of their gaze upon each other.

"Karissa, Nate is the man of the hour. He is turning the dirty thirty today. Nate is...." She paused as she noticed that neither of them were listening to a word she said. Both stood staring at each other as if in a trance. Her friend looked as if she had seen a ghost, and Nate was practically drooling with his eyes. It was as if he had seen the love of his life.

Rachel looked puzzled as she put her hands on her hips and cocked her head to the side. "Umm, do you guys know each other?" She asked, clearly confused.

Nate cleared his throat and shook his head a couple of times, and Karissa fidgeted nervously as he spoke. "Ye-yes, I'm sorry, Rachel. Yes. I know Karissa. I know her very well." He looked back at her in a way that made her heart melt in her chest. He was bold in his admission and didn't care what Rachel or Karissa thought of it.

Karissa blushed beneath his gaze and forced her eyes in Rachel's direction, but a known force of her heart drew her attention back to him. All six foot three inches of him. His classic navy-colored suit was tailored to show that he had grown and matured over the years. She saw from his gold cufflinks, gold watch, and expensive shoes that he had done well for himself. She wasn't shocked at all.

Rachel was intrigued. Karissa knew that her friend used to have a crush on this co-worker of hers, but she was over that months ago. She wasn't concerned that Rachel was jealous, but she knew that her friend wanted answers.

"Yes, umm, Rachel… Nathaniel and I met back in North Carolina a few years back."

"Nathaniel." Rachel tested his full first name. She smirked sardonically at the easy way Karissa said his name. Nate looked from Rachel back to Karissa, unbothered and amused.

"Four years to be exact," Nate shot back in an assertive but gentle way. He allowed his gaze to caress Karissa's face, interrogating her with his eyes.

Nathaniel's voice was husky with emotion. Karissa's heart could have exploded in the intensity of the moment. Glancing at Rachel, she saw her friend looked as if she was in the middle of a steamy soap opera. Karissa would have laughed if the knot in her stomach wasn't holding her at bay.

"OK—well, do you guys need me to step away or something?" Rachel asked. She was confused about what was unfolding before her eyes and felt she was imposing on an intimate moment. Yet, the way she focused on the scene was proof that she was in no rush to leave them even if they wanted her to go.

"No, stay!" Karissa said, grabbing Rachel's arm before Nate had a chance to respond.

Nate kept his eyes on Karissa and smirked at her eagerness to remove herself from his presence. Just then, a group walked over, pulling Nate into boisterous birthday wishes and embraces. He reluctantly broke his gaze from her to acknowledge the loud vivacious group.

Rachel turned to Karissa, her eyes large with curiosity.

Karissa kept a firm grip on Rachel's arm and pulled her away from the loud banter, clearly trying to find a way to escape before Nate's eyes could find her again. She glanced back as they made their way through the crowd. Just as she had expected, Nate was peering through the group surrounding him, and his eyes danced when he spotted her.

"Rachel, can we go, please?" Karissa asked desperately when they got to a quiet corner away from the crowd.

"Karissa, what is going on? I had no clue you knew Nate, and what is this? The way you two were looking at each other. What in the world?" Rachel said, confused and delighted at the same time.

"I will tell you everything. But can we go please, before he comes over here?" Rachel seeing her friend clearly in distress, nodded her head. "OK, fine. We can go." Rachel saw no eligible bachelors anyway. The men were either with dates, not her type, or just a little too thirsty for her liking.

* * *

Nate hadn't heard two words his friends said since they interrupted the moment with Karissa. He could not bring himself to believe what had happened. Was that Karissa Sparks who stood before him just seconds ago? It must have been a dream.

"Nate," his co-worker Darlene nearly yelled, drawing him out of his thoughts. "Sorry ladies, I apologize," he said with a charming smile. Alaina, his other co-worker, looked over her shoulders at the women dashing out of the room.

Nate tried to pretend he wasn't fighting the urge to chase after them. "So, how are you guys enjoying the party?" They turned their attention back to him. He noticed the way Darlene's friends stared at him, and a muscle jerked in his jaw.

"Who was that, man?" His buddy Julian joked playfully, punching him in the arm. "She your long-lost love or something, bro?" Julian continued, laughing with some other co-workers. The others laughed as they made light of the moment. Nate coughed at their directness and accuracy. Julian had become like a brother to him. He could tell when something was going on whether he recognized exactly what was happening or not. The others snickered at his embarrassment.

"Are you guys going to clown me at my party?" He gave Darlene and Alaina a sly, warmhearted look while cutting his eye at Julian and the other guys.

"Look, I wanted to introduce you to my friends." Darlene used her hand to sweep the air as if she was on a stage. "This is Tamara, who I told you about before. We grew up together, and she's in town for the week."

Nate could inwardly feel his reaction to Tamara's beauty and reprimanded himself. Karissa had not even walked off five minutes ago. He hated how his flesh always tried to rear its ugly head.

"Nice to meet you, Nate." Tamara stepped closer. "Happy birthday" she held her hand out to him. Nate took her hand but willed himself not to allow his eyes to sweep her body as he knew she wanted him to do.

"Yes, Nate, happy birthday, big head," Alaina teased him. He cut her a playful look. "Yeah, yeah, yeah." They both laughed as he turned his attention back to Tamara. "Don't mind these nuts. Thank you, and nice to meet you." He let her hand go rather quickly, just to make sure she didn't have a reason to misunderstand his friendliness.

Alaina started talking about how lovely the decorations were. Julian and the other guys excused themselves to get more food. Others around him began talking to each other about the music. Nate's mind drifted back to Karissa. He searched the crowd for her, but he knew if she was anything like she used to be, she had run. *Lord, she is more beautiful than I remember. Is this the answer to my prayers, Lord? Is this the time?*

At that moment, Nate was interrupted by the MC's voice over the mic. "Where is the man of the hour?" Loud applause and shouts of celebration broke out as he excused himself to head to the front. His emotions were raw, and he had no clue how he would make it through the party. He had never thought he would see her again, even though he secretly hoped for it—even prayed for it.

What was he going to do now? It took all his ability to not chase after her. That was something he used to do when they were in North Carolina. Karissa was a runner. She tried to break up with him every time she got scared or anxious—about anything and everything. He loved her so much even back then. Back when he was lost himself so much so that she had become an idol. He was drawn to her beyond what made sense to him. She was broken, and unsure of who she was back then. He knew this could not have been a coincidence. If God brought her back, He must have a plan.

CHAPTER 5

The Mother

Brenda woke up with a throbbing headache. There was an explosion of pain every time she opened her eyes. She heard sirens, voices in loud conversations she couldn't fully understand, and chaotic noises everywhere. It was all too much for her aching head.

She smelled a stench of urine so pungent she gagged as she inhaled. She felt she could just throw up right where she lay, but her body ached too severely for even that exploit. Her frail lungs seemed to collapse as she struggled to drag in each breath. She covered her nose with the sleeve of her jacket.

Where am I? she thought to herself as she continued to fight the heaviness that made her eyes almost impossible to open. The sun, muted by a cloudy sky pierced her eyes, making her regret her attempt to open them in the first place. She was outside somewhere that much was obvious. She rolled over in an effort to pull herself up and was greeted with a firm but concerned voice, "Brenda, wait, let me help you."

She immediately recognized her friend's voice. "Lucky," she said with a sigh of relief. "You're still with me. Where am I? What's going on?" Brenda asked in short quick breaths. It felt as if her ribs were on fire. The concrete beneath her seemed to claw at her.

Lucky came around within eyesight, grabbing Brenda's arms in an attempt to help her up. She could see that Lucky looked as bad as she felt.

"My goodness look at your face," Lucky bellowed with an unmasked spark of fear and alarm.

Brenda felt as bad as she apparently looked, she thought. She attempted to laugh at herself, but the pain in her side stopped her before it could escape her lips.

Brenda struggled to her feet, allowing Lucky to assist her even though she outweighed Lucky by at least twenty pounds. Once Brenda was to her feet, she forced both eyes all the way open in rebellion to the pain that seemed to burn deep within them. She touched her face where the pain throbbed near her temples and slowly dragged her hand to her right eye. Her face felt foreign to her. There was a knot near her temple and a puffy eye that sent a shock of excruciating pain to the back of her head. She cried out in a muffled tone, not wanting to draw attention to herself.

"Don't touch it, Brenda. You'll make it worse. Here take this." Lucky stammered.

Grabbing Brenda's arm, Lucky used her boney hip to support her. Knees buckling, Brenda used the support and tried to brace herself.

Once stable, Lucky reached down and grabbed a half-full bottle of water. Reaching into her soiled pant pocket, she pulled out two pills and handed them to Brenda.

Brenda opened her hand to receive the unidentified pills, cocked her head back, and tossed them in her mouth. She opened the flimsy plastic bottle and took a long drag of the water. The lukewarm sensation calmed the burning in her throat. Every bone in her face ached at the movement. She didn't ask what she had just taken, and at this point, she didn't care. She just wanted the pain to stop.

Brenda realized they were in "The Valley" the moment she slowly began to look around. Every movement had a price, pain, and she wanted to collapse but knew if she did, she would not get back up. She noticed the prostitutes stretched out by the dumpsters, their bodies exposed. She saw the addicts searching the ground looking for drugs. Slowly but surely, her mind began to flood with memories of last night's shenanigans.

"Last night was something else, I tell you," Lucky slurred. "I guess Ron and Mike got upset when you wouldn't have sex with them or something. They were drunk as I don't know what," she continued dramatically as she tried to keep Brenda steady with a firm grip under her arm.

"Yeah, it's a haze, but I remember," Brenda responded. She tried to take a step and groaned. Lucky tightened her grip. She remembered being at Ron's house with some of her people and others she didn't know.

"Ron brought Mike in and wanted you to spend the night with him. Said something about the punk letting him off the hook with a business deal gone wrong," Lucky explained, looking from side to side as if she was afraid that Ron would walk up any minute. "We're getting too old for all of this. I told you to make sure the jerk was in a decent mood before we got over there. You're gonna make me have to kill somebody."

Brenda shuddered at the memories from last night. "Yeah, I should have left when I saw Mike walk in. That was my fault," she winced. "He has had his eye on me for a while. I just didn't think Ron would do that to me." Brenda's eyes moistened.

"It's not your fault, honey. Ron is a scrub. It doesn't matter how much drugs he's given us. He's a snake and has always been one," Lucky barked as she scratched at her arm, which was red with a rash.

"He's not all bad all the time, Lucky." Brenda defended not just Ron but her weakness to the control he had over her.

"Ninety percent, just round it up. You give him too much control over you. You don't owe him your body or mind just because he gives you heroin and me crack here and there." She exaggerated the "here and there" part—it was more times than she wanted to admit. "We don't need the coward." Lucky loosened her grip on Brenda's arm. "Besides, Lionel is much better for you anyway if you ask me," she continued.

"Yeah, but Lionel won't give you crack, now will he?" Brenda said, touching her sore jaw. She knew Lucky put up with Ron for the same reason she did. Lionel, with whom she had a less complicated relationship, wasn't going to let her friend smoke up his stuff.

Besides, Ron never wanted her to be with other men. Last night was just different. She remembered her and Lucky smoking in the backroom of Ron's condo while music blasted from the living room. Brenda was the only addict allowed to hang in Ron's condo. Most addicts didn't know about that particular spot. Just the dope boys who ran for Ron and other men who stopped by periodically. Brenda chose to mind her own business. She had learned throughout the years of dealing with Ron that it was best not to ask questions. The more you know, the more likely you were to end up in a place you'd regret.

Lucky began to walk, leading Brenda out of the alley. There was a pleading voice calling out to her. "Brenda... Brenda loan me five. I got you next week when my money comes in." Brenda turned her head painfully in Tonya's direction. She noticed the makeshift bed of blankets where she was curled up. Lucky gripped her arm tighter, and Brenda looked at her contemptuously. Brenda loved Tonya but hated what drugs had done to her, what it had done to them all. Lucky knew it was a lost cause to try and stop Brenda from going to the wretched woman, so she let her arm go. She watched the pained way Brenda made her way towards Tonya and put her hand on her hip to signal her protest. "Tonya is just a no-class junkie," she muttered.

Lucky often scolded Brenda when she gave Tonya her last dollar. "We're all addicts, Lucky. Who are we to judge her?" Brenda always retorted. But Lucky despised her. Tonya was turned on to drugs by an ex-boyfriend just a year ago. And after three months of her addiction, she had lost everything. She used to be a buyer for one of the largest automotive companies in the Mid-West. She had just about everything one could want. But now she lived on the streets.

Brenda reached in her pockets and pulled out all the money she had—ten dollars. She peeled off five singles, struggling to see them clearly. She got down and handed the money to Tonya. Brenda felt every movement and moaned in agony. Tonya's eyes watered as she tried to lift her head off her book bag.

Brenda bent a little more towards her and touched her face. "Tonya, you have to take better care of yourself. Where did your left shoe go?" she asked as she looked over and saw that the blanket left Tonya's feet exposed. There was a sock and worn-down gym shoe on her right foot, but only a sock on the left, and it had holes that exposed her toes.

"Brenda, I should be saying the same to you. Who did that to you? Ron? I got something for him, Brenda, I swear." It was a shame that the bruises had Ron's name written all over them.

Tonya was about ten years younger than her, she guessed. No more than a few years older than her oldest son Kendrick. If anything, she should be a better example to the younger girl. But she was no better than her.

"Don't worry about me. I'll be fine. You just get yourself together. Don't depend on any handouts. I've told you that. You are smart, Tonya. Figure something out, girl."

Brenda was in no position to be giving advice. She was an addict herself. But she had to say something. She heard of Tonya's suicide attempts and drug overdoses a few months back, and she wanted to offer her at least a thimble of hope.

"Brenda, come on," Lucky stepped forward and was done hiding her irritation.

"She's talking. Don't you have two bucked eyes in that empty head of yours?" Tonya belligerently yelled back. Her eyes looked as if they would jump out of their sockets.

Lucky nearly jumped down on Tonya. Brenda leaped up instinctively and stopped the fight before it got beyond words. The quick action sent a rush of pain down Brenda's side, and she gasped sharply. Both Tonya and Lucky were alarmed and stopped mid attack.

"Brenda! I'm sorry, what is it?" Lucky asked franticly.

Tonya was also to her feet, reaching for Brenda in a weak attempt to stop her if she fell. Brenda lifted the right side of her shirt where the pain licked up her side. She noticed the nasty bruise. She sucked in air painfully and put her shirt back down.

"Oh, my goodness, Brenda," Tonya swore with heat rising to her face as her dull eyes widened.

"Brenda, let's go now!" Lucky yelled, just as distressed as Tonya. If she could, she'd kill the rat herself. He thought he was so tough beating up on women and all. She doubted he'd ever try it with a real man. She knew Brenda was minimizing the pain she was in, and she was determined to get her out of sight before Ron crawled out of whatever hole he was in.

"Ahhh," Brenda moaned as she tried to stand up straight. "It's fine, yea, let's just go," she said, conceding to Lucky.

Tonya relented as she self-consciously tried to smooth down her ruffled black mini skirt. "Yeah, just get from over here, and when I see that clown, I got something for him," she said, turning a jumpy eye to the blade near her dingy backpack.

Brenda knew Tonya was not bluffing and gave her a beseeching look as she glanced from her to Lucky. Ron frequented The Valley looking for her or when he needed to get a message to someone who ran dope for him. He rarely got out of his car, but everyone in The Valley knew when he was around.

Lucky rolled her eyes at Tonya's gesture and gently took Brenda's arm, placing it around her neck. "Yeah, yeah, don't get ya'self killed trying to dish out any favors. Besides, you wouldn't be able to get near Ron if you tried. Spare ya'self, little girl."

"Lucky, please," Brenda begged, knowing that Tonya was genuine in her concern for her.

Tonya had more to say to Lucky. "You know what, Lucky, how about you go find your own life instead of running behind Brenda's. The only reason you're here anyway is that you can't get dope for yourself, so you mooch off her connections. You're a bum who has no life of your own." Tonya then sat down on her blanketed mat.

"Y'all just need to stop," Brenda said to Lucky. "You're too old for all of that anyway. And you know those knees would give out on you any moment," Brenda teased. "You know she's young. I don't know why you let her get to you like that."

"Yeah, young and needs her tail whooped," Lucky teased back. "Besides, you baby the wench too much. Giving her your last dollars so she can go smoke it up," she said, shaking her head.

Brenda stopped and pulled her arm free. "I think I can walk. I'll be fine. It's hurting me more with my arm like that."

"OK. You sure you don't want to just go to the hospital to make sure nothing is broken?"

"No, I'm fine. I just need to lay down for a second," Brenda said, wanting to give in to the weight of the world that seemed to be crushing her.

"Lucky, you got that money you owe me?" said a deep raspy voice behind them. Turning, they saw Chuck, a local drug dealer, and some other guys leaning against the wall, passing around a cigarette. Brenda felt nauseous at the whiff of urine, weed, and other foul odors common to The Valley. The smell thickened as they moved toward the opening of the alleyway.

"I got you next week, Chuck," Lucky yelled out, trying to catch up to Brenda. Brenda wasn't getting as far as she wanted with that nasty limp. "Brenda girl, slow down before you collapse out here 'cause if you do this time, I'm walking right over you cow." They both laughed.

"Why didn't we go to your grandparent's house or Cat's place, for that matter? I don't even remember going to The Valley," Brenda said, slowing her pace as cars cruised down the street.

"Well, we got dropped off there after Ron nearly beat you to death and kicked us out. I was too high to protest, and I didn't know what kind of shape you were in because you were nearly unconscious, but saying, "Leave me alone." I thought you were also just high and needed to sleep it off. I was too scared to call the ambulance because we could've both been arrested."

"Yeah, I see," Brenda said heavily.

The weather was beautiful for a fall day in Chicago. Brenda allowed the sun to warm her face although she felt the pain. It was too early for much activity on the streets. Still, they did notice the local dope boys making exchanges with some desperate addicts. The addicts were digging nails into their arms, unaware if the itch was on their skin or in their souls.

She noticed everything. When she was sober, she saw herself in them, and it made her sick to her stomach.

"Brenda, I think you should go to the hospital. Seriously." Lucky noticed the way Brenda strained to see through her swollen eye. Yes, Brenda was about six years older than her, but that didn't matter. Lucky was protective of her and stepped in often because she felt Brenda was sometimes a little too fragile for the life she was living. You either stood tall, or you got trampled.

Whenever Ron got violent with her, Lucky would sometimes jump in to help if she was around.

"No, I'm not going to a hospital, Lucky. It's just a swollen eye and bruised ribs. I'll be fine. But I tell you, this will be the last time he put his hands on me." Her face froze in determination. "I'm tired of this crap, Lucky. Aren't you?"

Lucky shook her head in agreement. This was how Brenda got whenever she hit a low. That's where their lives seemed to rest these days.

Brenda was still going on and on about being done with this lifestyle when they arrived at Lucky's grandparents' home. When they opened the door of the small two-story home, the smell of tobacco and old furniture made Brenda sick to her stomach.

Lucky yelled out to her grandparents. It was funny because her voice did not rise to the level of a whisper. She was hoping they wouldn't respond. When no response came, she darted to her room with Brenda fast on her heels. Lucky had lived with her grandparents ever since she lost her house over five years ago. She hated it here as her grandparents loved to throw her addiction in her face, telling her that she was just like her mother, who had overdosed on cocaine thirteen years ago. Lucky had nowhere else to go since the rest of her family turned their backs on her years ago after rehab "wasn't the cure," as they often put it.

"Lucky has to want it for herself," others said. She was tired of hearing everyone else's opinion of her life. She hated their judgment. They could all go to hell for all she cared.

"Here, put this on your eye before you have people crawling out of their skin," Lucky exclaimed. She handed Brenda a frozen bag of vegetables she had retrieved from the kitchen freezer.

Brenda grabbed the bag and flopped across Lucky's full-size bed; her eyes closed facing the fading white ceiling.

Lucky watched Brenda, admiring her natural beauty even with a swollen eye, and busted lip. Brenda had the most beautiful curly hair that fell down her back whenever it was done-up properly. She usually wore it in a messy ponytail at the top of her head—which is how she had it now. Her skin was milk chocolate brown that had lost some of its vibrancy due to the drugs. Otherwise, the drugs seemed to have little effect on how Brenda looked, besides the yellow-stained teeth and her sunken eyes.

"You got something, Lucky?" Brenda asked after ten minutes of lying in bed like a dead person. "My head is killing me. I just need one hit," Brenda said with her eyes looking straight at Lucky.

"Brenda, you need to rest. I don't have anything anyway. Ron took everything he gave us when he threw you out." Lucky knew that her friend was not referring to over-the-counter medicine for a headache. They could only go a few hours here and there before they got the desperate urge for a high. But even those few hours seemed like an eternity. They were at the point where all they could do was stay high, long for the next high, and search for ways to get their next high.

Brenda began to fidget, and Lucky couldn't sit still either. She paced the room, walking in and out of the room every ten minutes.

"Brenda, have you thought about finding your kids lately?" Lucky's eyes darted around the room restlessly. That's the effect crack cocaine had on her. She could never be still. "You cried for them again last night in The Valley. You mentioned something about fear for your girls being raped. What did you mean by that? If you can even remember yourself."

Brenda's breath caught, and her heart jumped at the mention of her kids. Her eyes watered, and she looked suddenly angry. "No," she responded harshly. "I have not tried to reach them. I say crazy things when I'm high, and you know that. My children don't want to be found. I'm sure they want nothing to do with me. And I'm in no place to see them anyway. I can't have them see me like this," her voice broke.

Rebellious tears rode down Brenda's cheeks. She slapped them away as quickly as they came and groaned at the pain. She refused to allow herself to mourn. What right did she have to be sad? She was the one who lost her kids to the system. She was the one who screwed her life and her kids' lives up. She would not allow herself to be pitied. She deserved to hurt, deserved to drown in the guilt she refused to release. No, she wouldn't think about her kids. When she did reminisce about them—think about holding them, loving them, kissing them—she felt she could die. That's what she often wished the drugs would do—end her misery.

Lucky knew she could only get information about Brenda's children when Brenda was high. And she didn't know what to do with what little information she did know.

CHAPTER 6

Husband and Friends

Dr. Phillips arrived at the office early Monday and went to her desk to quickly review the files of her three scheduled clients. She felt an intense urge to pray for each of them. Kneeling on the carpet in the center of the office, she began to pray for them with fervor. When she started to pray for Karissa, her heart quickened.

She took a deep breath and filled her lungs with the sweet smell of vanilla that permeated the room from her candle. "*Father, what are you saying to me concerning Karissa? What do you desire to do in her life? Who is she really?*" Amanda asked all in what felt like one breath.

She waited a moment to hear what the Holy Spirit would reveal to her heart. She felt an overwhelming sense of love for Karissa, so much that warm tears dampened her cheeks. "*Father, please reveal yourself to Karissa. Remove every barrier, every obstacle, and every fear that would cause her not to know you. You are a merciful God. Please have mercy on Karissa, Lord. Whatever she is battling, expose it during our time together. According to your word—'With man, this may be impossible, but with God all things are possible.'"* She paused and allowed the response to warm her.

She dabbed away the tears streaming down her face with cool fingers. She sniffed a couple of times, determined to catch her breath. She didn't want to have to reapply her makeup.

She lifted her head and peered out the window. The sun seemed to beam joy upon her, and she allowed it to strengthen her for the day. Looking upward, she thought about the goodness of God in her own life. She prayed especially for Karissa—that she too would experience it.

She learned some basic things about Karissa during her first visit. She considered it a successful session because the young woman was completely skeptical when the session started. Only during the last twenty minutes of their session did Karissa share about her move to New York. She talked about what had brought her here, her time away at Brookdale University in North Carolina, and how much she loved her college experience.

There was also a love interest before her move, but she wouldn't go into detail. Amanda was satisfied that Karissa felt open enough to share what she did, but she knew they had a long way to go.

Amanda's phone rang. She was startled and almost spilled the coffee on her desk. She shook her head, slightly annoyed.

She looked for her bag. It was coming from the closet near the door. She went for it, wondering who could be calling her this early on a Monday. Her husband had her work number, and her daughter should be in class. She didn't give her personal number out to her clients. *Who in the world is it*?

When she finally made it to her phone, she saw a missed call from her husband.

She walked back to her desk to return his call from her work phone. She didn't like to be on her cell phone during the business hours she dedicated to her clients—he knew that. Just as she sat down about to click on his name to call him back, she saw a text pop up from him. Amanda loved her husband and loved it when he called or sent random messages. But today, she was a little on the edge, wondering why he had called her cell phone. She swiped right and opened the message.

A smile etched its way to her face as she read it out loud. "Hi sweetheart. Sorry to call your cell phone. I meant to call your work number. I was just thinking of you and wanted to say that I love you with all my heart. As I was praying today, you came to my mind, and I wanted to say that your clients are blessed to have you! Check the side pocket on your purse."

Amanda's heart swelled as she followed his instructions. She pulled a folded piece of yellow-lined paper from her purse pocket and ran her fingers across the black ink. "You may not get recognized often, but God sees your heart and you will be rewarded. I am proud to be your husband, and I am praying for you as you cover your clients today. Can't wait to see you later."

He ended the message with a winking face, and her face lit up as it always had with him.

She shook her head and said a silent prayer thanking God for her husband, Daniel, and asking Him how she got so lucky. And immediately felt a response in her heart, *not lucky, blessed daughter—the blessing of the Lord makes you rich and adds no sorrow*. The verse she loved so much in Proverbs chapter ten was on a sticky note in her bathroom.

She smiled a smile of gratitude and turned her attention again to her client files.

* * *

Karissa sat at her desk absent-mindedly, reviewing her part of the group presentation for a potential high-profile client. They had been trying to get this account for over a year, so she wanted to make sure everything was perfect. She loved her job as a marketing consultant at Push Marketing, one of the top advertising firms in New York City.

Her office overlooked Midtown Manhattan, giving her a view of the picturesque skyline that harmonized with the sky's brilliance. She turned in her seat to take in the sight as she often did when she felt overwhelmed. She snugged in her plush cashmere cardigan and allowed it to warm her.

As she scanned through the presentation making minor corrections, she was distracted by thoughts of what happened over the weekend. Her heart fluttered as she saw flashes of Nate's face. If there was anything more bizarre and unforeseen that could have happened, she couldn't think of it. She couldn't stop thinking about what had taken place at Rachel's random "co-worker's birthday party" that just so happen to be the guy she fell in love with over four years ago. It almost felt like she fell into a trance and couldn't shake herself out of it.

She told Rachel everything on their way back to her house from the party, and Rachel could hardly believe it. She had asked Karissa every question from, "What made you leave him?" "What more could you ask for?" "What were you going through?" "Do you still love him?" "Why haven't you told me about this before now?" The questions lasted all weekend.

On Saturday, Rachel and Sariah came over, and she had to re-live the entire night over again. Sariah, who had walked with her through the whole relationship and break-up, understood what Nate's resurfacing meant to her.

"Can you believe 'Risa wouldn't even give the guy her number or let me give it to him? I mean, what's the harm in being his friend. Nate is a great guy," Rachel exclaimed to Sariah as they sat on Karissa's couch eating ice cream.

"I'm sure Nate would never want just to be Karissa's friend. He was in love with her. I doubt he has gotten over her, or if he ever will."

They talked over Karissa as if she wasn't there. She was too tired to debate with them. But she had objected to Rachel's suggestions letting her know that she had moved on and "was not interested in revisiting the past." Rachel wanted Karissa to give Nate a chance, but she decided to let things take their natural course.

At her office desk, Karissa placed her hands on her temples, and massaged the ache as she slowly inhaled and exhaled deeply. *OK, girl, get it together. Finish this presentation so you can leave.*

She couldn't wait till two-thirty for her appointment with Dr. Phillips. She decided she would leave early on Mondays to make it through the Manhattan madness before the after-work chaos began. Her office wasn't too far from the therapist's office, and she was grateful for that. It was strange how she loathed the idea of seeing a therapist. Still, she secretly looked forward to it—especially today.

Mid-thought her phone began to vibrate on her desk. She reached to grab it, flipping it over to see who was calling. She saw Sariah's face pop up as an incoming FaceTime call. Karissa relaxed at the sight of her friend's name. She wondered if she should wait until she was finished with work before answering but decided she could use a break from her thoughts.

"Happy Monday 'Rissa! What you up to?" Sariah jubilantly exclaimed with her bright smile, causing Karissa to relax a bit.

Karissa always laughed when Sariah asked her what she was up to during work hours. "Girl, I'm working. It's Monday! You?", she shot back jokingly.

Karissa looked toward the door as if someone was going to come in. Placing her phone against her computer, she fumbled with the files on her desk, picking them up and stacking them in no specific order.

"Trying to figure out what Brandon has planned for the weekend," Sariah responded. Karissa noticed the way her friend blushed at the mention of her boyfriend. "I think my parents are trying to have a get-together at their house for their anniversary on Saturday. It looks like all the sibs and their families will be coming. I don't know how big it will be this year since dad hasn't been feeling well, but something small will be good for him." There seemed to be an unsettled look on Sariah's face, but she decided to let it go.

Karissa loved Sariah's family and felt they were her family as well. Except Sariah's youngest brother Benjamin had the biggest crush on her. The oldest brother Jacob used to have a crush on her too before he married. "Ah, I so respect your parent's love. It's been thirty-one years now that they are celebrating, right?"

"Thirty-two, and yeah, they are the cutest."

"So, what's the latest update with your dad?"

"Well, they have to put a stent in his heart and have to make some major changes to his diet. Mom isn't taking it so well, but my dad is hopeful."

Karissa's heart dropped at the mention of a heart procedure. Mr. Blake was the strongest man she knew. She couldn't imagine his heart failing.

Sariah placed her hand under her chin, holding the phone in the other hand. She was trying to contain her emotions.

Karissa saw that Sariah was in her office. Sariah pulled her glasses off and caught the tears that ran freely. Turning her full attention to Sariah, she tried to comfort her. "I'm so sorry, Sariah. I know that your dad will pull through this. He is the strongest man I know. He will be OK." She hated to see her friend this way.

"I believe as well," Sariah sniffled and sat up a little straighter in her black office chair.

A call came in on Karissa's phone that she did not recognize, and she ignored it.

"Anyway, you want to come to a small group with me tonight?", Sariah asked.

Karissa could see the hopeful look in Sariah's eyes.

Drawing her gaze from Sariah's, she put her attention back on the presentation on the computer.

"Nah, I'm good. You know I love you Sariah, and I appreciate you for always wanting me to be included. But I told you I can't go back to that small group. It's too much for me." Karissa paused, holding her breath. She didn't like the thought of potentially hurting Sariah's feelings.

"Why do you do that, Karissa?" Sariah pulled the phone closer, more attentive.

"What?" Karissa asked, uneasy.

"It's OK if you don't want to attend, you know I'll respect it. But why do you avoid what you're actually feeling about it? You look away or change the subject instead of sharing what's truly bothering you."

Wrapping her arms around herself defensively, Karissa scrunched her face. Exhaling deeply, she could see that Sariah's feelings were hurt. Why did she have to start this while they were both working?

"Sariah, look, if your God is real, He doesn't listen to people like me. I prayed with all my might that He would intervene many times when I was younger. It didn't help anything. If anything, things got worse."

"What got worse? What happened? You never shared it with me..."

She saw tears in Sariah's eyes and hated that she was the cause. "Look, I have to get back to work." Karissa's head began to ache.

"OK, but promise me you'll at least think about it. I know how you feel, and I also know how you can bottle things up and not deal with them." Sariah paused. "Oh, speaking of bottling things up, you have your appointment with Amanda today, right?" Sariah asked as if she almost forgot.

Hearing Dr. Phillip's first name with such familiarity felt strange to Karissa. She placed the phone against the computer again. She opened her desk drawer and pulled out her hair tie, gathering her hair and pulling it into a bun at the top of her head. "Yes, it is. And I'm looking forward to it, believe it or not," Karissa said as if she was proud of her response.

When Karissa finished the call, she leaned back in her leather desk chair and breathed deeply. Sariah was so sensitive sometimes. She thought back over the day she met Sariah at Brookdale University. It was their sophomore year, and Karissa was living a fast life. She had a group of friends that she hung out with consistently, whom she met during freshman move-in week.

When Karissa got to college, she wasn't focused on being a stellar student. She just wanted to be away from where she had come from in Indiana. She wanted to be free. The crowd she attracted were not the scholars but the cute popular girls whose only concern was knowing the right people and getting into the right parties with the right guys.

Karissa was present for every shindig, but she always felt out of place with them. She would look around at the lifestyle she was living – partying, drinking, and having sex with different guys. She felt she was drowning underneath the weight of her unhappiness. She refused to acknowledge her depression. She didn't have the time or liberty to entertain anything debilitating. She often thought of negative emotions as a threat to her ability to survive.

"If I allow myself to sit in depression and sadness I will get trampled. No one has time for that," she often told herself back then.

One day, she was sitting in the cafeteria by herself, waiting on a couple of friends. She saw Sariah and about three other students walking around the cafeteria passing out flyers. That wasn't the first time she saw the overly friendly girl in a group of friends passing out flyers about who knew what.

Brookdale was a predominately white school or "PWI," as they called it, so any black student or other minority groups were easy to spot. Sariah, while unassuming, had a natural beauty about her. She often dressed in jeans and a basic organization t-shirt most days. She was full of something that seemed light and child-like. Karissa watched her from afar from time to time, wondering who the bright-eyed, smiley-faced girl was, and wondered why she always seemed to have so much energy. But Karissa never bothered to acknowledge her and decided that she would mind her own business. That is, until that day Sariah walked over with a huge jubilant smile on her face. "Hi, my name is Sariah, what's yours?"

Karissa looked up from her phone and tried her best not to look bothered by the disruption.

"Hey, I'm Karissa," she said flatly. Sariah didn't look bothered at all by her disinterested greeting. She handed her the piece of paper she saw her handing out on multiple occasions. Karissa reluctantly took the blue piece of paper without looking at the content. She put it on the table. She said "thanks" with a blank look and turned her attention back to her phone. She didn't give Sariah a second look.

Sariah stood there for a long uncomfortable moment. "OK, well, Karissa, it was nice to meet you. We have a campus Bible study every Wednesday at 7:30 PM. I think you would enjoy it. Come out if you have time."

Sariah began to walk away. Karissa exhaled a breath of relief, but before she could get the full breath out, Sariah turned back. "Oh, by the way, you are really pretty. I'm sure you hear it all the time, but I just wanted to say so myself. I would also like to be your friend. I see you around all the time, and I see you are always with people. But I know how it is to be in the midst of a crowd and still feel lonely." With that, Sariah walked away, continuing to pass out flyers to the frolicking students at the other tables.

Karissa felt her heart in her stomach. She had never had someone speak to her that way. Like they knew her all her life and could really see her.

Karissa hadn't even noticed she was crying until a couple of her friends walked up with a look of grave concern on their faces. "Karissa, what in the heck happened?" They exclaimed as they sat down.

Karissa wiped the tears from her face and shook her head. "Oh nothing, it's nothing," she said quickly. Although hesitant, her friends knew that Karissa wouldn't open up, so they changed the subject. At that moment, Karissa knew that she would love Sariah, and no matter what their differences might be, she would definitely be her friend.

CHAPTER 7

The Break

When Karissa made it to the Interfaith Counseling Center, she greeted Ramona, the receptionist, signed in, and took a seat in the waiting area. She checked the clock and saw it was 3 PM. She relaxed a bit into the cushioned chair. It was still working hours, so she understood that the silence closing in on her was due to the time of the day, not the lack of need for therapy.

"Mrs. Sparks, would you like something to drink? Water or tea?"

Karissa smiled at Ramona. She guessed she was from somewhere in South America based on her features and accent.

"It's Ms., but Karissa will do just fine. And no, thank you," Karissa said a bit uneasily. She shifted in her seat, angling herself towards the walkway where Dr. Phillips would appear.

The woman looked embarrassed as she stared at her from behind the desk. "Oh uh, I'm sorry. I hope I didn't offend you. I should have paid better attention to the intake form," Ramona said.

Karissa smiled a forced smile. "It's fine," she said, quickly turning her attention to the clock on the wall again.

Why did the acknowledgement of her marital status make her uneasy? She pondered it in her heart. It was the assumption that she wasn't single. She had no ring on her finger, but somehow people always assumed she was married. It made her feel self-conscious, and she hated it. She decided to put those thoughts and feelings out of her mind for the moment.

She picked her phone up from her lap and opened Facebook. She scrolled mindlessly, passing the time. Hearing heels click-clack, she turned her head towards the sound and saw the same woman from her last visit. She sat up straighter and crossed her legs.

This time Karissa had no hat to hide under. Instead, she had her big curly hair placed in a bun on top of her head, a white button-up shirt, and a pair of nicely fitted black slacks. She wasn't quite sure why she was so self-conscious about being in a therapist's office. It was the twenty-first century, for crying out loud. Everyone was seeing a psychologist or therapist of some sort.

She stared at the petite woman as she stopped at the reception desk. The woman had no tears spilling from her big blue eyes this time, but she still looked despondent.

Karissa fidgeted in her seat, resting her head on the palm of her hand, trying to look as if she was minding her own business. When the woman began to walk in her direction, Karissa tried not to make eye contact. She could feel the presence of the woman right in front of her.

Karissa looked up nervously with questioning eyes.

"Hi, I saw you last week, and I'm so sorry if I seemed rude. I was having a rough day, and..." The woman shook her head, waving her hand dismissively. "Never mind all that. You didn't come to hear about my problems." She laughed more to keep herself from crying, it seemed.

Karissa tried to look as attentive and empathetic as possible, "No, please. You didn't come off rude at all. My name is Karissa. Nice to meet you."

Karissa held her hand up to the woman awkwardly. She wasn't sure if she should get up from where she sat or not. She felt weird to be sitting down, looking up at the woman. It made her uncomfortable.

"I'm sorry, where are my manners. My name is Sam. Samantha, but everyone calls me Sam," she spilled out in a nervous stutter. "Well, it's nice to meet you, Karissa. I assume you're here to see Dr. Phillips?" Sam asked, looking at Karissa with a glimmer of hope. Karissa nodded her head smiling in an attempt to mirror Samantha's.

"Well, Dr. Phillips is the best, so you are in great hands. She has been an angel in walking me through my divorce. Whatever you are seeking, the Lord will use her to help you get there." Sam smiled genuinely at Karissa.

"Well, I'm not seeking anything in particular, just testing it out since a good friend of mine recommended it. But it's good to talk to someone trained to listen. I'm also not really into religion, so not sure how much the 'Lord' can do for me. But I look forward to seeing where this goes," Karissa said as politely as she could.

While Samantha's kindness touched her, she was a little annoyed with her bringing up God and insinuating that she was seeking something. *Why did she have to be seeking anything? Why could she not have just come to talk and express herself to someone?* She thought to herself.

Samantha looked puzzled, and her face wrinkled a bit, but she quickly caught it and smiled instead. "I understand. Either way, I know your time will be lovely, I'm sure," she turned her head, glancing at the elevator door. "Well, I have to go now, but hopefully, I'll see you next time Karissa!" And with that, Samantha stepped toward the elevator.

Karissa waved goodbye and relaxed a bit more. She wondered how Samantha could still believe in God when she was going through a divorce.

"Ms. Sparks," a voice called, interrupting her thoughts. She looked over and saw Dr. Phillips near the reception desk. She had a smile on her face and waved a yellow folder in her hand, inviting her back.

Again, Karissa admired the neatly placed bun to the back of her head and her gray pinstripe pantsuit. She had light makeup on, and Karissa could see her natural beauty.

"Hello, Dr. Phillips. Good to see you again," Karissa said warmly, offering her hand.

"Yes, Karissa, lovely to see you again," she said as she shook Karissa's hand gently. Dr. Phillips led the way to her office. Karissa saw that the other doors were closed with "Do not disturb" signs hanging on the doorknobs. She noted that while the office was quiet, there were still appointments taking place, which made her not feel as alone.

Once in Dr. Phillips' office, Karissa again felt a strange peace come over her. She relaxed more than she thought possible only a week before. Dr. Phillips sat down and opened the file that was in her hand.

Karissa sat across from her in the recliner. Looking around, Karissa noted the brightness of the office. The sun was beaming through the large window, and it reminded her of the cheery brightness of her own work office. The office had the same intoxicating smell as before, which slightly mimicked the waiting area's fragrance. It was a much warm-er scent. Karissa felt at home. However, she still intended to keep up her guard since she didn't want Dr. Phillips to feel comfortable enough to overwhelm her with an agenda.

Karissa's head began to swim with anxiety as she thought about the question she was asked during her last visit: Why she was there? What she looking to come from her visits? The truth of the matter is that Karissa wasn't sure what she wanted. She wasn't sure what she was seeking. She understood that she had a traumatic childhood, but she wasn't ready to discuss that. Being honest about her past meant facing the fears that lurked within her. She only wanted to focus on her future and what it had in store for her.

Karissa thought, and had even confessed to Sariah, that she felt there was more to life than she was living. Yes, she had the job she wanted. She loved marketing and helping businesses grow their brands and ultimately increase their revenue and profits. She loved where she lived and was satisfied with her social life. She had people in her corner like Sariah and Rachel, who loved her just the way she was. While she wasn't married at twenty-eight years old, she had what most would consider a successful life.

Sitting back in the chair, Karissa rubbed her sweaty palms on her dark slacks and took deep, measured breaths. She tried to be inconspicuous as she tried to slow her beating heart. What was this? She felt panicked.

Looking up from her notepad, Dr. Phillips interrupted her thoughts, "OK, Karissa, how are you doing? How was your weekend?"

Karissa zoned back in. She was silent for a few moments thinking over her weekend and allowing her heart to slow. She started moment by moment from Friday. She spoke gingerly about Rachel's "co-worker's" birthday party that just so happened to be for her ex-boyfriend/nearly fiancé's—the event that almost turned her world upside down. She hadn't seen or talked to Nate in years. She had not expected ever to see him again. And there he was, standing before her as if a dream and nightmare collided right before her eyes. She saw flashes of his magnetic smile and deep brown eyes. He had become even more handsome since she last saw him, and she wasn't sure how that was possible.

She was stunned that he still looked at her the way he did back then. She assumed he should have moved on after all these years. But, according to Rachel, he was single. Many thoughts fought for space in Karissa's mind as she shared the encounter.

All the while, Dr. Phillips looked on with wonder and amusement as Karissa fluently shared one moment after the next. She noticed that Dr. Phillips took notes as she talked, and she wondered what she was documenting. Karissa even shocked herself about how open she was being. She had never felt so at ease talking to anyone, not even Rachel or Sariah, about matters that touched her emotionally. She wondered for a moment why it was so easy to talk to Dr. Phillips, but she continued despite the lingering doubts.

Karissa talked about the dream that persisted throughout the years. "I've been having this same dream for years…" she looked down, wringing her hands together tightly. "I'm always running through an old familiar home, trying to locate a screaming girl." Karissa paused as her heartbeat wildly. She could feel the attentiveness of Dr. Phillips's gaze upon her. "I can never make it to her," she confessed. Heat flooded Karissa's face as she felt the hot tears sting her eyes. *Pull it together Karissa, what is wrong with you?* She was horrified and confused that she had revealed so much.

"How often do you have these dreams?"

"Multiple times a month. Sometimes multiple times a week."

"I see," Dr. Phillips began to write in her notepad.

"How does this dream leave you feeling?" While it was apparent to Dr. Phillips that the dream aroused some deep emotions in Karissa, she wanted her to reveal more. Looking up with veiled eyes, Karissa shrugged. "I don't know." She felt angry with the question.

Dr. Phillips gave her a knowing look. "I understand. How are you feeling right now in this moment as you recounted the dream? I know this may be a frustrating question—asking about emotions, but it will help us to unlock the meaning of the dream."

More than anything, Karissa wanted to know what it meant. She exhaled a deep sigh and looked back down at her hands. The air around her became heavy.

"I'm usually panicked in the dream. The girl sounds frightened and tormented. I feel some sort of strange connection with her—as if she is..." Karissa paused thoughtfully, "a part of me." She shifted in the recliner. "I may feel uh... sad and hopeless when I wake up. Maybe because I can never reach her," Karissa shrugged again.

"I think this dream is something to unlock," said Dr. Phillips. "I won't dwell on it now since we don't have much time left. But I want you to write out this dream in all the detail you can remember. Write down the look of the house, the smell, and even how you feel when you awaken from the dream. We will come back to it next week."

Closing her notepad, Dr. Phillips looked up and smirked. "Well, Karissa. You had quite the weekend, I'd say." Karissa chuckled slightly. That took the edge off, and she was grateful.

"Yes, I guess you can say that," Karissa remarked rather sheepishly.

Dr. Phillips tucked back a strand of hair behind her ear and pursed her lips. "Here is the thing, we want to discover, Karissa. We want to discover and unlock who you really are.

We want to understand how you got to where you are to understand how to get you where you want to be. It is a process of discovery."

Dr. Phillips paused to choose her words carefully. "I know that you are not a believer in Jesus. You know that I am, so we don't have to beat around the bush there. I will respect where you are, however. While I have academic degrees dealing with the human mind and emotions through behavioral science, I believe it all originates with God. So, a lot of how I think comes from my relationship with Him and my understanding of the Bible. I will do my best to help you without crossing boundaries, but I need you to trust the process. I would love to be a support for you on your journey, if you allow it."

Karissa swallowed hard. *She pities you* is the message she heard from within her mind. She exhaled as Dr. Phillips finished her last statement. Dr. Phillips leaned in, waiting for Karissa's response.

Karissa didn't know what to say. She was prickly all over with fear at being invited into the unknown. Yet, at the same time, she was strangely touched. She knew that she wanted the help Dr. Phillips offered. She sounded so sure and confident, and a hunger burned within Karissa. Even though she didn't know what help she needed— she felt that Dr. Phillips might, in fact, know. But a louder, more sardonic voice told her to run. Her face hardened, and defensiveness washed over her.

"Dr. Phillips, I do appreciate your genuine offer to help me..." Karissa picked up her cross-body black leather purse from the side of the recliner and smoothed nonexistent wrinkles from her pants. "But to be honest, I am not on a self-discovery journey of where I came from, or how I got to where I am now. I am not interested in digging through my past to discover anything. I don't want to waste your time or my money. I did enjoy seeing how Sariah had more clarity on her future after her sessions with you, but Sariah and I are different. Very different. So, I do apologize, but I don't know if our sessions are going to work for me." With that, she began to move towards the door quickly.

"Karissa, I apologize if I have made you uncomfortable." Dr. Phillips was shocked and confused by Karissa's statement. She got up from behind the desk and walked swiftly to catch Karissa before she reached the hall.

Karissa stopped just short of reaching for the door. She looked back over her shoulder as Dr. Phillips hastened towards her.

"Karissa, I want you to know that my office is always open for you if you decide you would like to continue where we left off." Dr. Phillips held her arms out as an invitation of embrace.

Karissa was again shocked by Dr. Phillips's kindness. She could see Dr. Phillips wanted to say more, but chose not to. The offer of a hug almost caused Karissa to weep. But she refused it and thanked Dr. Phillips one more time before leaving the room.

She held her head down as she walked down the hall towards the exit. She nodded at the receptionist as she tried to ask Karissa how her session went. Karissa hated being rude, but she would give in to the tears that so eagerly wanted to be released if she opened her mouth. She had paid for her session online and was grateful she had thought ahead so that she wouldn't have to stay in the office any longer. The receptionist must have caught the hint and stopped mid-sentence as Karissa waited impatiently for the elevator. She would go home and forget that she had ever tried such a pointless endeavor.

CHAPTER 8

The Prayer

Amanda kept replaying the abrupt ending of her session with Karissa. The burden was heavy on her mind and soul, and it showed in her demeanor and expression. It was late afternoon, and she still had one more client to see, so she knew she had to pull it together.

She rarely responded this way, even with the most extreme cases. Yes, she prayed for all of her clients constantly, but something was different about Karissa. She had been a therapist for years, but there were only a handful of cases she could remember when she felt the way she did now. It was like God had entrusted her with a burden she knew wasn't her own. How was she supposed to be a part of God's larger plan when the young woman was so hardened? She had opened up so much during their session—what made her close up at the end?

"Lord, how am I supposed to be obedient to you in Karissa's life when she ended our sessions? Your ways are not my ways, nor are your thoughts my thoughts. I asked that you give me

wisdom and understanding. I just want to please you, Lord. Where do I go from here? You have spoken to my heart, and I ask that you also speak to Karissa's heart too." Her head came up quickly, and she grimaced in a stark realization. She knew the enemy was behind Karissa's abrupt decision.

Amanda felt a sudden urge to call her husband. Opening her desk drawer, she retrieved her cell phone. She touched the FaceTime option when she found his name and tried to smile as she waited for him to accept her call. His face chased out her anxiety and caused her to relax in the chair.

"Hi baby, how are you? You OK?" Daniel asked, clearly wondering about the nature of her call. Yes, they always texted each other with no agenda except to say "Hi," or "I love you," but he still worried when she called if it wasn't lunchtime. But hadn't he mentioned earlier that she was on his mind while praying?

"Yes, I'm OK," Amanda answered with a bit of sadness in her eyes and tightness in her throat.

"You don't look OK. What's bothering you?" There was a knock at Daniel's office door. He lowered the phone, "Hold on sweetheart." "One minute," he said.

She shifted in her seat, feeling bad about interrupting his day. She heard him giving an employee instruction on a construction project contract documents they were presenting to a client. She adored how her husband ran his company and how he so attentively managed his staff. Daniel owned a small construction company. Well, they both owned the company, but Daniel ran it. When he first started five years ago, she had quit her job to help him get things off the ground. They both quickly realized that she was better at doing what she was passionate about—what she was created to do. She was created to help people get from a place of hopelessness and brokenness to a place of freedom and wholeness.

Daniel, on the other hand, was a businessman. He was excellent at it and enjoyed employing men who needed a second chance in life. He hired men with felonies and men who were ostracized by society for one reason or the other. She loved that about him. His heart was so big, and he not only employed these men, but he mentored them in life.

She checked her watch—she only had twenty minutes before her next appointment. She saw him lift the phone back up until his face was completely in full view.

"OK, babe, I'm sorry. You were saying?"

"No, I'm sorry to call during your busiest time of the day," Amanda said in a dejected tone.

"Amanda, you are my priority. You're not a bother to me, and you know that. So, tell me what's on your mind?"

Amanda's heart skipped a beat at his boyish grin. He was so handsome with his well-groomed salt and pepper beard. They had been married for seven mostly wonderful years.

They would soon be celebrating year eight on his birthday. Daniel would be turning thirty-eight in just a couple of months. He had always been an old soul despite his age.

"I just wanted to hear your voice and have you pray with me for one of my clients." A rebellious tear slid down her cheek, and she quickly swiped it away, not wanting to worry him further.

"Amanda, what is it? What's the matter?" Daniel asked, looking as if he wanted to jump through the phone. He sat back further in his chair, showing her that he was in no rush.

"Well, it's crazy that I'm reacting like this because I don't really know this young woman. She is a friend of Sariah, so I have a little context about her. From the day I met her, I've had a heavy burden in my heart for her. It's almost hard to explain it. It's just…" Amanda choked up again.

"It'll be OK, Amanda. You've had moments like this before when the Lord gave you a burden like this for someone."

"I know," Amanda said, this time grabbing a tissue from the Kleenex box at the bottom of her desk drawer. "But this one is the heaviest I've felt. Today she ended our sessions because she wasn't ready to talk about 'feelings.'"

Daniel rested his head on the back of his chair, placing his right foot over his left leg the way he commonly did.

"Her pain is so tangible I can feel it myself. I sense that there's a very special call of God on her life. She seems so lost and alone."

Amanda exhaled as if the statement exhausted her. "She's not a believer. Not yet anyway," she smiled somberly.

Daniel stroked his beard, hanging on Amanda's every word.

"OK, well, it seems like the Lord is showing you that she needs you. So, let's pray continuously for her. The Lord will make a way for His plans to come to pass, and we just need to do our part."

Amanda's alarm chimed, signaling five minutes until her next and final appointment for the day. "I have five more minutes until the next appointment," Amanda said as she re-adjusted the phone in her hand.

"OK, let's pray now, and then we can talk at home." They both bowed their heads, closing their eyes, and Daniel prayed quickly but passionately.

He told her he'd pick dinner up, and with that he ended the call. Amanda felt a weight lift and peace return. She silently thanked God for her husband as she gathered the files for her next appointment.

CHAPTER 9

Help for Brenda

Brenda heard people speaking on the other side of the door, so she knew that people were in the house. She banged louder and more impatiently than before. She didn't want to alarm the neighbors. The big homes and expensive cars made her feel out of place. She had walked nearly ten miles, and her feet were on fire. She shifted impatiently from one foot to the next as she tried to smooth any frizz from her ponytail. She wanted to look half decent, although she didn't feel decent at all.

Brenda was nervous whenever she had to come here, but she had nowhere else to go. She could only stay with Lucky for a few weeks at a time without Lucky's grandparents kicking her out. Lucky's grandparents were kind people, but they had become intolerant of their grandchildren, especially since her grandfather had fallen ill. Like her brother, Lucky had turned to drugs, shaming their family the same way their mother had done. Only their grandparents maintained a relationship with them. They allowed Lucky to stay with them knowing she was an addict, and her brother also came from time to time.

Brenda also stayed with Angie, her self-proclaimed aunt. Angie was not Brenda's biological aunt but was a friend of her mother's before she passed. Angie had helped take care of Brenda since she was seventeen years old.

Brenda lived with her grandparents before that. Her grandmother died when she was fourteen years old, and her grandfather followed three years after that. They left the house to Brenda, and she stayed there with Angie stopping in to help look after her.

Her grandparents were the last relatives she had outside of Josh and his wife Sheryl, or at least as far as she knew. She had been on her own for the most part. A flash of her mother's sweet smell and warm embrace ached in her memory. She was only five when her mother died.

Brenda's grandparents became very distant after her mother passed away. They didn't read to her like she remembered her mother doing. They didn't hug her like she remembered her mother doing.

She remembered very little of her father, who was killed by "gun violence," shortly after her mother died, from what her grandparents had told her. She had never known any family on her father's side.

Her grandfather took Brenda to school until she was sixteen-and-a-half; and then her he taught her to drive and bought her a car. He would often tell her, "I won't be here forever, Brenda. You are gonna have to learn how to take care of yourself, you hear me? Life ain't no crystal stair for any of us. You gonna have to learn to survive fa' ya' self, you hear me?"

And she would answer ruefully, "Yes, papa. I hear you."

Finally, Brenda heard the door being unlocked in response to her pounding. It jerked her from the nostalgic memories.

"Brenda." Her cousin looked at her stone-faced.

"Josh, Hi. I…" Josh walked off, leaving the door open with her standing there. She hated herself for having to come here. "Well, hello to you too, Josh," Brenda exclaimed in a tone doused with hurt and anger.

"You haven't seen me in a year, and that's how you act?" she said with a sting of pain in her voice. She was used to her cousin being this way. Though it was hurtful, she couldn't blame him for treating her this way. She had stolen from him many times when she was in severe need of a high.

She met Josh after her grandfather passed. He was fifteen years her senior and was the son of her grandfather's late brother.

"Brenda, how are you, honey?" She heard the tender voice coming from the kitchen. She closed the door behind her and reluctantly sat her bag down as she braced herself to greet Sheryl, Josh's wife.

She watched as Josh stormed up the stairs angrily, shaking his head and swearing under his breath. He was in his sixties, but he had the build and stamina of a forty-year-old. He had an athletic body and was over six feet tall. He had aged well over the years, and his shaved head made him look even younger.

"Brenda, don't you mind him. He is an angry old man. Come here." She held her breath to keep from crying. She looked at Sheryl, who was as radiant as ever. She was a heavyset woman with the loveliest brown skin and warm smile.

Brenda fell into Sheryl's welcoming embrace and almost didn't want to let go. She smelled like sugar cane and maple mixed with something citrus. She must have been baking cookies or a cake. How long had it been since she was embraced this way? By someone who loved her just the way she was. Knowing who she was and what she had become.

If Sheryl ever loathed her, she never expressed it. "What happened to you, Brenda? You look as if you've been beaten. Do you need to go to the hospital?" Sheryl asked with concern and wide, worried eyes.

"Thank you, Sheryl, but no, I'm fine. Just a little incident. It's no big deal," Brenda said coolly, not wanting to draw more attention to her problems. It had been a few days since her altercation with Ron, so the swelling of her eye had gone down, yet it left a nasty bruise.

Sheryl looked as if she wanted to protest but decided against it. "Here, I'll take your bag. Have you had anything to eat?"

Brenda was self-conscious about her pillowcase of a bag. Josh and Sheryl were not vain people at all. Still, they were well-off since Josh ran the technology department for a large health care company in Chicago. Sheryl was a Licensed Clinical Social Worker. It was a vocation that grew from her innate love of people and her desire to help them.

Sherly moved about the kitchen, gathering a glass of water and a tray of muffins, and placed them before Brenda. Pausing, her plump hands gripped the edges of the kitchen island. "You were about the same condition as you're in now the last time I saw you. All beaten up or what have you. Brenda, you're going to have to leave these streets alone. God's hand is on you, but you may not always come out with just bruises." Brenda noticed Sheryl's hand shaking when she moved one from the counter to lightly touch her mouth.

"I know, I know. Really, it's not all bad, Sheryl." She paused to stop the wave of grief from pouring out of her eyes.

"It really was bad. I remember even if you refuse to remember. You nearly scared me half to death—and Josh too, even if he won't admit it. He tried to find the guy for days after you left."

"It's just Ron and his temper. He don't mean no harm, really. I can handle him myself. No need to fuss." She took a sip of the water allowing the coolness from the glass to calm her.

Brenda didn't want to be reminded of the incident. She was too high and didn't want to go to a hospital. Lucky had someone drop her off at her cousins' place, where they forced her to go to the hospital. After only a few days of being in their home, Brenda had stolen all the cash in their bedroom drawer, which totaled over two thousand dollars, as well as some jewelry from Sheryl's jewelry box. She hadn't seen them since.

Josh shut down, wanting nothing to do with her. Sheryl seemed to love her even more. She couldn't understand it at all. Sheryl would often say, "Love covers a multitude of sins, dear."

It was well after 10 PM when Brenda finished eating and catching up with Sheryl.

"Brenda, what's your plan? You can't stay here without a plan. Aren't you tired of living the way you've been living, honey? You've lost everything, your grandparents' home, your children…" Sheryl caught herself at that reality.

Brenda looked off so that the death grip on her heart wouldn't stop it from beating. Her wandering eyes noticed that they had remodeled their kitchen. There were stainless steel appliances, marble countertops, and beautiful luxury flooring. It wasn't that she hadn't paid attention to these things before, but she took a special interest in it now—anything to escape the question at hand.

"Brenda, look at me," Sheryl sternly demanded.

Brenda lifted her head as if it took energy she didn't have.

"When will enough be enough?" Sheryl asked as tears streamed down her cheeks. She wiped them away as if the weight of Brenda's life took everything good out of her.

Brenda saw the gravity of her condition in Sheryl's face, and she broke down in a sob that crashed suddenly over her. Sheryl walked around the kitchen island and swept Brenda into her big plush arms as though she was a prodigal daughter.

"Listen to me, Brenda. I have told you this before, and I will keep telling you this until you finally get it," Sheryl whispered in Brenda's hair as Brenda's face fell unto her bosom. "This addiction is impossible with you. It really is. I get it. But with God, all things are possible."

"No, you don't get it. I can't stop Sheryl. I can't!" She yelled even though she had not intended to do that. "I have tried," she confessed. "You don't understand anything. Everyone thinks they know, but they don't," Brenda said, her sobs coming so quickly her shoulders jerked with the waves of them.

Brenda heard the sound of the stairs creaking and tensed up. She didn't want her cousin seeing her like this. She didn't want to see the judgmental look on his face. Then she heard the sound of someone going back up. He was the only one up there, she believed, so she relaxed a bit. He must have heard the commotion and wanted to make sure she wasn't doing anything harmful to Sheryl. She shrunk a bit more inside at the thought.

"I want to die, Sheryl. I just want to die," crying more hysterically until she had lost all control. Sheryl, trying not to leave the embrace, reached over to grab a piece of paper towel from the roll on the counter.

"You listen to me, Brenda," Sheryl said, her own tears blurring her vision. "Your life is not over. Do you hear me? As long as there is breath in your lungs, the good Lord still has a plan for you. This is not your end. Don't you dare give up." Brenda felt she already had.

My grace is sufficient for you, for my strength is made perfect in your weakness. The familiar verse boomed so loud in her heart that she stiffened. She hadn't heard that voice in a long time—she had tried not to.

Sheryl patted Brenda's back while flipping the flighty strands of hair from her brow.

The love Brenda felt was so sincere that she almost wished she could stay. Yes, she almost wished for it until it came back. The thing she felt she could never escape. The thing that she felt would torment her every day for the rest of her life, even during a seeming life-altering moment with Sheryl. She felt it invade the essence of her being and darken hope as if it never existed—the desperate need for a high.

* * *

Sheryl allowed Brenda to sleep in the spare room in the back of the house. There were nicer rooms upstairs, but she knew this was Sheryl's way of trying to keep her and Josh as far away from each other as possible. She knew she had no right to be picky. She was shocked that they had yet again opened their home to her.

Brenda closed the freshly painted door after Sheryl did the final check to see if she needed anything. The door was a crisp white and had the smell of wet paint, although it was dry. Brenda would have been comfortable if Sheryl gave her a sheet and told her to sleep on the floor. She was used to vile living conditions; whether it was Lucky's bedroom floor, Angie's twin-sized guest bed with sharp springs poking her on every side, on the pavement in The Valley, with Lionel in the rat-infested motel, or next to Ron—which was the worst of all. She appreciated when she had the chance to be with Josh and Sheryl, no matter how much Josh hated her.

She stood by the door taking in the decent-sized room. The floors were new as she remembered that this room used to have carpet. Now the wood felt cool against her thin worn-out socks. She had removed her shoes at the door, as was the custom of everyone that came into Josh and Sheryl's home.

The bed was full-sized, similar to the one she used to sleep in upstairs. There were pictures on the wall that she didn't remember seeing the last time she visited. There was minimal furniture in the room other than the bed. There were the pictures, mint green curtains covering the windows, and a small nightstand with books on it. The lights were dim, but there was enough for her to see comfortably.

She sauntered over to the pictures, taking them in one by one. She didn't recognize a lot of the people and assumed they were Sheryl's side of the family. Unlike she and Josh, Sheryl had a huge family. She noticed Sheryl's sisters in one picture. It was taken at the beach with the sun setting behind them. They were teenagers or in their early twenties, she guessed. Sheryl was in the middle with her arms outstretched, so her sisters fit within them in a big inclusive hug. They all looked so happy and free in their swimsuits.

Next to that picture was one of Sheryl's parents. Her mother was still alive and had to be in her late eighties by now, Brenda thought. Sheryl's father had passed away some years ago from a sudden heart attack. Brenda remembered it as if it had happened yesterday. It hit their family hard because Sheryl's dad was like a father to everyone he met. He was something different altogether—a real jewel. Her parents were picturesque as they looked at one another with the love of young lovers with forever to go.

She didn't recognize any of the people in other pictures. She looked deeply into the faces of a family portrait with eight to ten people in the photo, but she did not see a familiar face. There were several pictures of children during milestone birthdays, but she didn't know any of them. Suddenly, her eyes fell on one photo that took her breath away. Could it be who she thought it was? She blinked her eyes and looked closer. It was a picture of her mother and father kissing under a mistletoe.

She moved in even closer to take the picture in with all of her senses. She wanted to touch the image, smell it, and taste it with her eyes. She felt a wave of sadness come over her, and she couldn't believe what she was seeing. She had never seen this picture before. She hadn't seen many photos at all in her grandparents' home growing up. It was like they wanted to forget that her mother even existed so that they wouldn't have to acknowledge the pain of their loss.

Brenda saw herself in her mother's features—she had beautiful curly hair that touched her shoulders, smooth brown skin, and a curvy shape. Her mother was enchanting.

She peered at her father. He towered over her mother at roughly six feet four inches. He had a low cut with wavy hair and dark chocolate skin. They were quite the vision. Her eyes were plastered to the picture as if there was a magnetic force drawing her in. She hadn't realized she was crying until she felt the coolness of the tear that hit her forearm.

Brenda's mother, Kimberly Lyles, and Josh were first cousins. They were close before she passed away—at least that's what Sheryl shared with her years ago. Brenda didn't have any memories of Josh when she was young, and he didn't come around after her mother's death. He once told her that her grandparents pushed everyone away after they lost Kimberly. He said they were never the same after that.

Brenda resented her grandparents for keeping her away from the only family she had. She even suspected that they were why she didn't know her father's side of the family. She tried to locate them on her own a few times when she was in high school. She remembered trying to google their last name to see if any pictures of them would pop up. She even had her friend's kids search relentlessly on Facebook, without success.

Her grandparents told her that her mother never introduced them to her father's side of the family. They claimed they did not know if he had siblings or where his parents lived. She couldn't deny that even though she despised her grandparents, she also pitied them. They were alone and broken. She understood her grandparents now more than ever. She knew now what it was like to lose a child. While her children were still alive, or at least that's what she had hoped, she did, in fact, lose them. She lost them to the foster care system. She might as well have lost herself that day.

Everything felt like death—every day, every memory, and every breath. All the memories came back in what felt like an ocean of grief and torment. Brenda exhaled the pain of it all. Only the pain didn't escape with her breath. The pain clung to her heart, her mind, and threatened to dissolve her into nothingness.

She forced herself to pull away from the picture. It took all of her might to do it. Before she thought better of it, she walked back over to the wall and pulled the photo from the collage. She stared at it, allowing it to satisfy her hunger for a high. She walked over to her bag that lay limp on the floor by the bedroom door and slipped the picture in it. She decided that she would take it and one day make a copy of it and return the original to Sheryl and Josh.

She couldn't look at the rest of the pictures. The photo of her parents had taken all the energy she had left. She pulled out the only piece of nightclothes she had from her bag—a long yellow nightgown that had turned a brownish color. She peeled the clothes off her body and replaced them with the nightgown. She flicked the lights off and headed to the bed, hoping she would be able to sleep.

Brenda tossed from side-to-side as sweat beads began to roll from her forehead to the soft cotton pillow. She grabbed at herself in an attempt to calm the aching in her bones. She hurt all over. It grew from a hollow ache to a feeling that someone was pounding on her entire body. She cried out in desperation.

She had become accustomed to the withdrawal symptoms, but they never got easier. Her body violently attacked her resolve to reject heroine with every passing hour. She needed one hit; her mouth watered as she thought about it rushing through her bloodstream, relieving her of her misery.

Rolling out of bed, she stumbled in the dark to her bag. If she could just find a little something to help her relax, she would be fine.

Pulling the rags of clothes out, she threw them wherever they landed. She searched the corners and the sides of her bag and found nothing. She fell back on the palms of her hands and allowed her body to collapse on the floor. She cried, silently grabbing at her hair. Getting up from the floor, she walked to the door turning the cool knob slowly, trying not to wake Sheryl and Josh.

She tiptoed down the hall, her eyes glued to the floors. Maybe she had dropped something when she came in. She rubbed her arms as the ache gnawed at her. She saw nothing. She needed to look harder. Getting on the kitchen floor, she searched earnestly around the island where she and Sheryl were sitting. Her knees ached in rebellion, but she continued searching. She found nothing. Maybe she could fight this once and for all. Maybe she could kick the addiction and find her kids after she did.

Getting up, she walked back to her bedroom. It hurt to walk, and the pain would not allow her to stop thinking about getting high. Maybe she should look around for something Sheryl and Josh wouldn't miss and sell it. She didn't notice anything that would go easily unmissed. *Think Brenda*, she scolded herself.

She could fight this. She was tired of living this way. Or she could die—whichever came first. She plopped back in bed, warding off the chills creeping up her spine. She gripped the sides of the bed as her head began to throb, causing her to become nauseous. It seemed like her bones were being crushed, and she moaned louder than she wanted. Or at least that's what it felt like— a breaking of her being.

She heard heavy footsteps hastening down the stairs as she let out a desperate cry for help, "Ahhhh, please help me please," she screamed.

The door slammed open without a knock of warning. "Brenda, what is it?" a breathless Sheryl heaved out. She flicked the lights on and hastened to her side with a look of confusion and panic.

"Withdrawal," Sheryl said. She laid a warm hand on Brenda's forehead. Brenda closed her eyes in an attempt to shut out the world and the pain.

She heard Josh's voice and was surprised to hear worry. "She's having withdrawals," he said matter-of-factly.

"Yes," Sheryl said as she looked over her shoulder at him. She had a pleading look in her eyes that signaled him to keep any sly comments to himself. He held his hands up as a sign of surrender.

"We need to get her to a hospital."

"No, I just need one hit, and I'll be fine," Brenda said over clenched teeth. "Call my friend Lucky for me, Josh."

Sheryl's hands were now on her shaky shoulders. "Oh God, no!" Sheryl exclaimed.

"Brenda, you came to the wrong place if you think we're going to help you get drugs," Josh said in an agitated tone. "By God, you can leave now if you so please. Do you want to fight this or not?"

Sheryl shifted her body from the bent posture over Brenda to face her husband. He relaxed his tone. "Sheryl, she needs help, not pity. We can help her—I'm fine with that. But I will not coddle her," Josh said with finality.

"Yes, you are right, honey." Sheryl turned to Brenda in a posture that showed she supported her husband.

Brenda remembered times when they attempted to help her, but those times were slim to none after she lost her children.

Sheryl pulled back years ago when helping Brenda began to take a toll on her marriage. Brenda thought they had given up on her indefinitely, but maybe that wasn't true. Sheryl bent again beside the bed as Brenda held herself tightly. Her skin felt clammy under Sheryl's hand that rested on her cheek. "Brenda, do you want to fight this? Do you want to get well?" Sheryl asked sweetly.

Brenda had tears streaming down the sides of her face, and they spilled onto the pillow. "I know that you have tried to fight this before, but you don't have to do it alone. We will be here for you every step of the way if you want to fight this." Sheryl searched Brenda's eyes for an affirmative answer.

Brenda looked at her with childlike vulnerability. "Yes," she groaned, "I want to fight." With that, her body began to shake violently.

"Quick Josh, grab your things. She needs to get to a hospital now!" Sheryl said with tempered sternness.

Josh ran out at the command, and Brenda felt her body drowning under the pain.

CHAPTER 10

The Past

"You did what? Why did you do that?" Sariah questioned with intense distress.

Karissa sat on her couch with her legs positioned underneath her as she picked up her tea to take a sip before responding. Moving the cell phone closer to her mouth, she spoke with controlled determination. "I didn't sign up for someone to tell me how I'm going to live my life, that's why. I know everything you're going to say, so please, spare me."

Karissa exhaled, feeling overwhelmed. She could not deny that she knew there was something off about her response to Dr. Phillips. But she didn't feel like sorting through it all. She just knew she wanted to get away from her, far away.

"Karissa, please hear me," Sariah pleaded. Karissa could almost see Sariah's face as the words tumbled out. Sariah was likely pacing, her eyes dancing around the room where she was, soft-faced in an attempt to respond, "in love." Sariah continued as Karissa braced herself. "No one said it would be easy. Why did you quit so soon? You didn't even give it a chance. Besides, you just said that you enjoyed the session last week, right?" Sariah signed.

"I did, but today was just too much. I can't..."

"Karissa, please...you have to give it a little longer. Trust the process" she could hear Sariah's desperation, and she softened.

Sariah continued deliberately, "Karissa, you don't speak to your family. Your adopted family or biological family. You have shut people out, and that is just not healthy. You are having panic attacks and nightmares. You have to let someone help you" she heard Sariah pause at the weight of her words.

It felt as if someone threw a bucket of freezing water in her face. Sariah wasn't finished, and Karissa knew she should have just hung the phone up before saying something she would regret. She felt the heat rise to her face, and she couldn't get words out fast enough. "Who died and made you the judge of my life?" Before the response could come, she hung up the phone.

She sat back hard against the cushion of her couch, tossing the phone on her living room table. She heard the way the phone cracked against the glass and regretted her fit of anger.

She glanced outside her living room window seeking to distract herself from the swirling emotions rising inside of her. It was a brisk October evening, and she felt a slight draft seeping in from the large window of her sixth-floor apartment. The sun nowhere in sight, just the dark cloudy sky hovering over the city and her life. Taking a deep breath, she used all the strength she had to gaze upon the majestic canvas where the clouds danced. She always loved the mystery of the sky. It seemed to be a world in and of itself. She loved that the sky kept her life in perspective. She was small and insignificant compared to it. And just maybe her problems were insignificant as well.

Why did life have to be so complicated? She let her mind wander over the events of her day, and all that was weighing on her.

Yes, she willingly signed up for counseling but was she wrong for wanting to decide how her time was spent there? She was the one paying for the sessions, so why couldn't Dr. Phillips respect her desires for the use of their time together?

Karissa choked back tears she felt welling up inside her. What was really bothering her? She thought about these things as she sat Indian-style on her couch. She grabbed the pillow and hugged it against herself. She thought over her life, trying to locate her emotions and why they seemed to be going in a downward spiral. Everything seemed to poke at her nerves lately. She found herself blowing up over the smallest things. Why had she snapped like that on Sariah? She knew that her friend only had her best interest at heart, and she would never intentionally hurt her.

Karissa's face felt hot, and her head tightened with anxiety. Trying to "process emotions," as Sariah often put it, was just too much. She decided to focus her attention elsewhere.

Nate. She couldn't tell if that windstorm would destroy or revive her. Why had she run from him? All weekend she ignored Rachel's plea to allow him to have her number. She even saw that he found her on Facebook the other day. She had ignored his friend request.

Her heart felt warm inside and her stomach felt as if she took a drop on the rollercoaster. She remembered the way he looked at her at his party. It was as if she was the only one in the room—like she was the only one who mattered. Even when he got pulled into the joy and celebratory conversations with his friends, she saw him stealing glances at her. He looked at her as if she belonged to him, and as much as she rejected the possibilities, she couldn't deny that she felt it as well. She hated feeling as if she had no control of her life. She hated it with a passion that made her blood boil. She knew she needed to get up and prepare for bed, but she decided to rest on the couch for a while. She stretched out wearily and let the darkness pull her in.

Heart beating wildly while beads of perspiration pricked her forehead, Karissa frantically paced through the familiar house, searching for the voice that cried out to her. It was the voice of a little girl screaming, hypnotizing her consciousness. She ran deliberately down the hazy hallway until she saw the wooden door to the upstairs from where the cry was coming. There was a daunting smell that lingered in the house, exposing its unkempt condition. She took the stairs two at a time. The staircase seemed to have no end, but Karissa was determined to make it to the child.

"I'm coming, I'm coming. Please hold on, wait..." she yelled up the stairs in the direction of the cries. She panted like a deer with no brook. She stopped midway, bending at the knee and drew in deep long breaths. Her lungs burned, and she pulled herself up, catching her breath. Her heart caught in her throat as she looked up and saw a beast staring back at her. It was a creature she had never seen before. Screaming frantically with death gripping her soul, she fell backward down the stairs feeling a fear she had never known before.

Karissa awakened, gasping for air as her body convulsed. Panic-stricken and crying, she began to touch her face, moved down to her arms, and back to her face again.

Looking into the darkness of her apartment, fear closed in on her. She reached over hastily groping for the lamp on the stand. Shutting her eyes as the light pierced in, she placed her head in her palms and wept. Images of the grotesque beast flashed in her mind, and she gasped sharply, afraid to close her eyes again.

What was going on? What was happening to her? She tried to get herself together, but the tears were a never-ending stream. She aimlessly wiped the sweat from her face into her hair. Her mouth was cotton as she got up to get a glass of water from her refrigerator. She glanced at the time—9:40 PM. She knew that it was time for her to head to bed considering she had to be up early for work. Instead, she decided to take her glass of water back to the couch to process the dream.

The coolness of the water seeped into her body and calmed her. Resting her back against the couch, Sariah's words came back with loud, vivid aggression.

"Karissa, you don't speak to your family, your adopted family or biological family."

Her past was not a place she liked to frequent. She decided to let Sariah's words wash over her. Yes, it was true she had cut her families off a long time ago and had no intention of reconciling. She had many memories of her mother, but the most prevalent one was her and her siblings in the back of a police car being taken away. She was seven years old when the police showed up at the shelter where she and her siblings lodged. She didn't remember much about that day. But she remembered holding her little brother as he used his little one-year-old lungs to express his fear and confusion.

Her mother had left them in a shelter because she had to "go get them school supplies" for the upcoming academic year. And they believed her, because why wouldn't they?

Karissa's memories then shifted to her last week in Indiana before she left for college. She had received a call from her older biological brother, Kendrick. He let her know that he had found their mother and wanted her to come with him to see the woman who had abandoned them for drugs.

Karissa's heart leaped when her brother brought the news of having located their mother. They hadn't seen her in over ten years at that point. Karissa thought about her mom all the time. She would even write her letters when she felt the most alone. Yes, of course, she would go to Chicago with her brother to see her mom for the first time since they were taken from her. She didn't know what had become of her father. She was never close to him, even before they were taken into foster care. She eventually found out that he was the one that turned her mother on to drugs. Karissa took another sip of her water as she recounted the memories. Lying back against the couch she continued to remember.

Karissa was eighteen years old when they set off to locate their biological mother, and Kendrick was twenty years old. She was nervous when her brother pulled up to her friend's house to pick her up. Kendrick was adopted by a different family who was a lot more liberal than the family that adopted her and her other siblings. He mentioned to her during their conversation that he told his adopted parents where he was going. He was an adult, but he still lived in their home while he attended a community college nearby.

On the other hand, although she was eighteen years old, she had no such liberties. She didn't get along with her adopted family and couldn't wait to escape to North Carolina for school. She had only a few more months before graduation. She told him to pick her up from a friend's house because she didn't want her family asking questions about where they were going.

He told her he ran into an old friend of their mother's that he recognized at the mall one day. Karissa was always amazed at how much her brother remembered. Even though she and her brother grew up in different homes, they remained the best of friends. He pulled up in his shiny red drop-top with the biggest smile on his face. It was a picturesque spring day in Indiana, and her nerves were causing her stomach to cramp. During the ride, she daydreamed about what their reunion would be like.

She imagined they would pull up to a big house and that the doors would swing open as they arrived and that their mother would come running out with open arms panting with joy. She hoped she would apologize for losing them and share how she had been clean from drugs and ready to start a relationship with them.

Karissa remembered her heart ached with longing that day. Her brother was silent the entire ride, and she assumed he was doing the same thing—dreaming of the possibilities.

"I remembered him. He was a friend she used to have back in the day. He just gave me the address," he had said with a big smile and shrug. He had no phone number, so their visit would have to be a pop-up surprise. She assumed that after all these years, their mother had to be in a good place, and maybe they would even be able to find their father as well. Her young heart beat wildly thinking about her family coming back together again.

"Oh my gosh, Kendrick, can you believe after all these years we'll finally see her? I'm nervous, but more excited than anything. What do you think she'll say?" Karissa blurted out as they rode down Sunset Blvd., where she had spent most of her adolescent years. It was a middle-class neighborhood with just the right amount of drama and harmony.

"I don't know, 'Rissa, but don't get your hopes up. She was a crackhead at the end of the day. They don't clean up so easily."

Karissa had cringed at his bluntness. "Heroin Kendrick. Her drug was heroin," Karissa stated rather dully since her levelheaded brother decided to kill her mood.

"What? How do you know?" Kendrick asked, both shocked and amused at his sister who seemed to know way too much all the time.

"I overheard one of the foster agents talking about it when we were first taken." She drew in a long breath before continuing. She despised the way they spoke of her mother and made a promise to herself back then that when she was old enough, she would give them something to gossip about. "The woman who was cleaning us up mentioned to another caseworker that 'their mama is a heroin addict and will probably be dead in two months.'"

Kendrick looked at her alarmed that she had heard such talk at the foster care agency. But they had seen and heard far worse before.

When they pulled up, her brother looked from the address on his phone to the motel to make sure he had put the address in correctly. They were both looking around in confusion and perplexity. Where were they? And why were they at a motel? The GPS didn't identify the location as a motel. As they looked around, they saw the sign above the entrance was worn down and hanging off the pole with the name faded.

They looked around in confusion and unease. Their mother's old friend didn't give them a room number, so they pulled up alongside a woman who staggered aimlessly towards one of the rooms. She was disheveled with her mouth hanging to one side, hair matted to her head, and clothes falling off her.

Kendrick pulled over and asked the woman if she knew a Brenda Lyles. The disoriented woman, slurring her words, directed them to the first door beyond the motel's entrance.

They thanked her and nervously pulled into one of the parking spots directly in front of the room.

Karissa suddenly felt that they should turn back around and go home. But her desire to see her mother was like something that yoked her to a mule, propelling her forward and wouldn't let her loose.

She remembered that Kendrick led the way as he swung the car door open in determination. He was a broad shoulder six feet three inches tower of confidence. All Karissa could remember was the butterflies that flew around wildly in the pit of her stomach. Her brother looked at her sheepishly, grabbing her hand and asking her if she was ready. Of course, she wasn't ready, she wanted to interject, but she would not be a coward. She slowly nodded her head, and they walked towards the dreadful unknown.

Karissa pressed back deeper into her cushioned couch, holding back the tears as the memories continued to flood her mind. Her mind trailed back to the day at the motel. Kendrick was the one who braved the fear and knocked on the faded red door which looked as if it had not been painted since the building was erected. She held her breath and closed her eyes afraid of what was to come. She opened them hesitantly after a few seconds when no one answered.

Kendrick looked at her with a fallen expression and slumped posture. Before she could open her mouth to suggest they leave, the door flew open.

Her brother released her hand abruptly as they both braced themselves. What she saw took her breath away and caused her to want to vomit. The smell of something foul mixed with fear gripped her lungs—she was repulsed.

"Mom?" she heard Kendrick say with a crack in his voice. Karissa turned her attention to the woman standing before them and she recognized her. Her head felt heavy as she turned to look at her brother. Her heart sank at the tears on his cheeks. Their mother was thinner than she last remembered, but you could still notice her curves. Her long curly hair lay lifeless on her shoulders. Her dull clothes hung loosely off her body.

Brenda stood there with tears in her eyes. She didn't speak. She nervously brushed her hair back as if she could will life into the limp curls. She tried to close the door a bit, hiding what was behind her as if her small frame could achieve such an impossible task.

At that moment, Karissa looked to see what she was trying to hide, and her knees buckled at the sight of it. There was a white woman and a seemingly short black man sitting at a small round table. The woman was completely naked, and the man had on nothing but boxers. They were sniffing something on the table with a rolled-up bill. Karissa looked closer and saw a white powder-like substance they were snorting up their nose. There was also a pipe and crystal-like rocks on the table next to them. Their mother realized they saw what was going on and walked out towards them, pulling the door shut as she did.

They both stood there cemented to the ground, unable to move or speak.

Brenda began to cry, and Karissa could see she was shaking. Her grief was mirrored in her mother's eyes.

"My God. My babies," Brenda whimpered brokenly. Kendrick was the first to step towards her with his arms out to take her in. Brenda hesitated, looking at Karissa with shame cloaking her as she pulled Kendrick in, fiercely kissing both sides of his face. She began to cry out that she was sorry. Kendrick wept in his mother's arms. They were holding on to each other for dear life.

Karissa looked back at the car, unsure whether to run or wait for her brother. She held herself, closing her eyes to control the river of sorrow flowing from them. It felt as if her world had crashed in around her and it threatened to choke the life right out of her. A rush of sadness washed over her at the realization that there would be no elaborate welcome with swinging gates and a sober mother.

"Karissa, sweetie," Karissa heard the desperate voice of her mother as Kendrick wiped his tears. Her mother held boney arms out, but Karissa couldn't move. Instead, she broke down, weeping uncontrollably.

Kendrick straightened and rushed to her side, and embraced her. She fell into his arms as she watched her mother turn around with her hand on her head, looking up with a pain that deeply struck Karissa.

Her mother was overtaken with a grief and sorrow that Karissa had never seen before. Her mother shook violently as sobs wracked her body.

Karissa straightened and walked slowly towards her mother. Brenda turned with a look in her eyes that Karissa would never forget. Her mother loved them in a way that she couldn't express in words, and Karissa saw it. She fell into her mother's embrace as if it was the last time she would see her. She cried in her mother's arms as Brenda brushed her hair with a warm, clammy hand, kissing her head and saying that she was sorry over and over again.

There was a distinct smell of something acidic, and her mother reeked of other strange scents. Karissa could still smell it in the back of her nose as she returned the present, laying on the couch in her apartment. The feel of strong hands of love too deep to comprehend and deep sorrowful eyes stuck with her. She tried not to remember those details, but they invaded her as if she were still there.

Karissa sat up straighter on her couch as she absentmindedly wiped the tears off her cheeks with the back of her hand. The memories were overwhelming. She reached over and took a tissue from the box. Grabbing her water, she took another sip and sat the cup back on its coaster. She grabbed her cell to check it, not looking for anything in particular. She saw the time –10 PM. She exhaled heavily knowing she needed to be in bed but still didn't feel like going to sleep. She looked out her window and smiled to herself. She loved living here. The luminous skyline across the East River was beautiful.

She went to her Facebook app and began to scroll through her timeline. She had only a little over one hundred friends since she decided to delete her old account and start a new one. She made the change a couple of years ago when she started to get friend requests from old friends and family. She didn't post on social media too often anyway but had friends who would post pictures tagging her, which told her whereabouts. She preferred that people from her past not know what she was up to now. She scrolled through some statuses of people complaining about different social issues, some jovial statuses begging for laughs, and some pretty funny memes.

As she continued to scroll mindlessly, a picture of Nate flashed in her mind, and her heart skipped a beat. She needed a distraction from her jog back through her hellish past. What harm could there be in just checking out his Facebook account, she thought to herself.

She went to the search icon at the top of the page and began to type in his full name first: Nathanial Rye. But only strangers popped up. *Why am I doing this anyway?* Karissa thought to herself but continued. She went back, deleted the full name, and typed in Nate, and before she could get the last name out, she saw it pop up as the first option. He must have changed it she thought. She saw his Facebook image, with piercing eyes, staring back at her. Her heart leaped as she nervously clicked to open his page, but careful not to mistakenly respond to the friend request.

She scanned through his info intently. She didn't want to click anything by accident. She looked to see if his timeline gave away any information that Rachel hadn't shared. His college listed as Rockford University, also that he now lives in New York, and she saw that he was single. She didn't understand why her heart leaped as if Rachel hadn't told her that already. But seeing it here made it real to her that he hadn't claimed another woman as his own.

She continued scrolling down his page, and saw they had fifteen friends in common, which didn't surprise her. Before she deleted her old page, they had almost one hundred friends in common. They knew many of the same people in North Carolina. Still, she had not added many of them back as friends on social media platforms. She did not want people asking questions about her and Nate after they had broken up, and she also wanted no reminders of him.

As she continued her scroll, she looked at the content of what he was posting. He had reposted a couple of status from pastors with words of encouragement. There were quite a few people who had reposted his statuses tagging him in it. One status caught her attention: "Jesus must be the center of any relationship for it to prosper."

She felt a sting of irritation rise up in her at the statement. She had seen many prosperous relationships where Jesus was not the center. The arrogance of his statement was why she despised the Christian faith. They thought their "god" was the end-all-be-all. She had seen many broken relationships with so-called "Christians" and had seen many great relationships with people of different faiths. They didn't need Jesus to have prosperous lives or relationships.

She clicked out of his page, put her phone in hibernation mode, and tossed it to the side of her. That's why she broke up with him in the first place, she recalled. He started to grow a friendship with a guy who was a respected minister in North Carolina near where they went to school. That's when her beloved Nate began to change.

Nate came to see her one day when he begrudgingly encountered this persistent young minister—she paused to remember his name. Samuel, she thought to herself as if a light bulb went off. His name was Samuel. One day, Nate told her that he had given his life to Jesus. He said that he wanted her to come to church with him and wanted her to get to know Jesus. She fumed at his audacity and laughed in his face.

"If you want to accept some naïve theory as truth, then go right ahead, but don't think I'm going to follow you in it," she said to him with hurt eyes.

She had loved Nate since she met him at a college football game one day. Her school was playing against his alma mater, and they had a close mutual friend. He looked at her then the same way he looked at her at his party a couple of weeks ago. As if there was no one else to him but her. But she would not be a fool for him no matter what. She would not blindly follow after a god who was said to be good and all-powerful while bad things had happened all her life. She wouldn't do that for anyone, not even Nate.

Karissa gave a big stretch and yawned, letting her fury subside. She had nothing to be upset about; she was not with Nate, nor would she ever be. Yes, she still loved him with every breath. But she would go on with life the way she always had.

Karissa grabbed her cup and turned off the living room lamp. She closed her curtains and took her cup to the dishwasher. Turning off the kitchen light, she headed to her bedroom to get ready for bed. She would put all the memories of the day away. Tomorrow would be a new day.

CHAPTER 11

Painful Recollections

Brenda hurt all over. Her bones seemed to be breaking in pain. Sweat soaked her sheets and seemed to cling to her. She forced her eyes open and looked around the stark white room. She noticed Sheryl sat at her side.

Brenda's teeth began to chatter as if she was cold, but the sweat soaking her sheets said otherwise. The room seemed to be closing in around her. She wanted to pull out the pain she felt in her stomach with her bare hands. Brenda groaned and turned her head to the side in agony.

Sheryl got up from her chair and bent over Brenda in a motherly way. "Brenda dear, do you want me to grab the nurse? Here, drink this," Sheryl said, grabbing the cup of water from the rolling tray near the bed.

Brenda grabbed at herself as she cried out in pain. At that moment, the nurse walked in with a calm that showed her experience. She came to Brenda's side and gave Sheryl an understanding look.

The nurse handed Brenda a small white cup with two white pills. She lifted Brenda up so she was positioned to take them. She gave her a cup of water and watched until the pills were down and Brenda was content.

Sheryl sat back down, exhaling deeply. She and Josh had used a connection they had to get Brenda checked into one of Chicago's top rehabilitation centers. Sheryl was between a rock and a hard place since she knew Brenda had been to rehab a few times before. It had changed nothing. She would make progress for a month or two and then relapse. Bad friends and old feelings always dragged her back to the dark place she had sought to escape. It seemed each time her addiction got worse. Sheryl said a silent prayer, wondering why she had done so much to get Brenda into rehab, knowing that she had failed many times before.

Josh told her that she was crazy to spend her time and their resources on his cousin. He told her it was pointless. "Brenda doesn't want to be free," he had said indignantly. She looked into her husband's eyes, wondering why he couldn't forgive Brenda for the choices she made in life. Yes, Brenda had hurt them many times; she had stolen from them, lied to them, and said a lot of hurtful things when they wouldn't bend to her will. But there was something different about this time. She tried to explain that to Josh, but he couldn't receive anything she had to say about Brenda anymore.

She felt that God wanted to use her as a vessel to set Brenda free from this addiction once and for all. She had seen recoveries in far worse situations as a social worker. If people had a will to escape and had support, they could do it. She knew in her soul that Brenda was not destined to remain in this condition for the rest of her life.

Sheryl sometimes couldn't explain her draw towards Brenda. She seemed to have a supernatural connection to her. She had never known someone with such a great heart but had been dealt a tough hand in life. When Brenda was much younger, she tended to be easily influenced. She wasn't the type to stand up for herself and allowed other people to make decisions for her too often. Josh would say she had no backbone, but Sheryl saw it differently. She was a sheep in need of a shepherd like everyone else. However, she always noticed Brenda's gentle heart. Drugs and life on the street almost always made people hard and sometimes impossible, but Brenda was different. At least that's the way Sheryl saw it.

Brenda had become more troubled in spirit after the death of her grandparents. Brenda took it hard when her grandfather passed away. She had already lost her grandmother a couple of years prior, and her parents when she was only a child. As if that wasn't enough, she was brutally raped by a Chicago gang member when she was eighteen. Sheryl believed that was the turning point. It was like Brenda ceased to trust the Lord, herself, or anyone else. Sheryl saw the decline begin, but she could not have imagined that Brenda's life would have come to this.

Brenda was smart and had wanted to go to college. She had a bright future, even with the trauma she experienced. She was always quick to learn a new skill and was great with numbers. With the supervision of her next-door neighbor, Angie, who had been like a mom to her, Brenda was able to stay in her home and finish high school. After high school, Brenda decided not to go to college right away. She said that she wanted to take a couple of years to live her life first. After graduation, she said, "I don't want to be a prisoner to school again."

At that point, Sheryl was not involved much in Brenda's decisions and would not stand in the way of how she wanted to live her life. She knew Brenda was wise beyond her years but still needed guidance. She saw that Brenda was more gullible than most due to her not having many relationships growing up. But who was she to get involved at the time? She and Josh had only come around after her grandfather passed. Other than that, they were absent from the girl's life.

Sheryl didn't want to come in and start playing her mother. Brenda was kind and sharp, but she wouldn't easily bend to direction. Sheryl and Josh tried to keep in touch with Brenda, but that was not an easy task. When Brenda began to have her children, they tried to be more present. Outside of the next-door neighbor, Angie, Sheryl knew they were all the people Brenda had in her life. She did not know her father's side of the family, and the family on her mother's side was deceased for all she knew.

Brenda was able to survive working a minimum wage job because of the inheritance her grandparents left her. Sheryl smiled at the days where Brenda was young, sober, and figuring life out. She didn't seem quite the same after the rape. They all were broken and devastated by such a deplorable attack. She wept for Brenda for months after that and questioned God. *Brenda was young and had already been through so much. Why did that have to happen to her?* Sheryl often asked in prayer.

Brenda had the most beautiful children, but something was not right with the children's father, Caleb Smith. He was a hard man and had done some time in prison—for Lord knows what— before he met Brenda. It was rumored that he had killed a minister he tried to rob. She never knew what Brenda saw in the young man. Sure, he was handsome and had money, but you could smell trouble a mile off. Josh would often say that something was off with Caleb mentally, but he couldn't quite put his finger on it.

Things didn't take a turn for the worse until after Brenda's third child. One day Sheryl received a call from Angie telling her that she had Brenda's children and had not seen her in days. Angie suspected Brenda had gotten into drugs and was squandering her inheritance with Caleb. She shuttered, thinking about Angie's panicked voice as she rehearsed the path Brenda was taking. Her children, Kendrick, who was six years old at the time, Karissa, who was four years old, and Sarah, who was one year old, were at risk.

Even with their father's disturbing ways, Brenda seemed to do a pretty decent job raising them from what Sheryl could see. She couldn't imagine that anyone could influence Brenda to start doing drugs. But then they all thought she would lose her fourth child, Caleb Jr., who was devastatingly born with a heroin addiction.

Sheryl was pulled from her memories when her phone rang. She fumbled with her purse in pursuit of it. She pulled the phone out, and a breath of fresh air seeped through her lungs when it read "husband" on the screen. She sent the call to voicemail and sent a hurried text back letting Josh know that she would head home now. She couldn't wait to hear his voice, but she didn't want to call him while she was at the rehabilitation center with Brenda. Yes, he was on board with supporting Brenda through her journey, but he didn't like how much time Sheryl was spending at the rehab center. She hadn't told him that she would be there today.

She kissed Brenda's cheek and told her she would be back tomorrow. Brenda opened her eyes, looking up at her in a child-like way.

"Sheryl, I will never have the words to tell you how much you mean to me, how thankful I am for you." Tears spilled down Brenda's face.

Sheryl brought a hand to her shoulder, but Brenda continued. "I am not worth it, I know. I've made a mess of my life, and I don't deserve your help. I'll never be able to repay you for believing that I could beat this addiction. Hell, I don't believe it myself. But I want to beat it, Sheryl. I do." More tears came as Brenda tried to continue.

Sheryl stopped her. "Dear, none of us are deserving of any good thing. The word of God tells us that no one is good. Not even one." She placed a hand on Brenda's cheek. "But thank God that He loves us despite ourselves," Sheryl said with beaming eyes. She looked at her with all the love she had. "Freely I have received, so freely I give," she said. And with that, Sheryl grabbed her lightly worn artisan leather bag and walked out the door.

Brenda couldn't think past Sheryl's kindness. Yes, her body hurt so badly she wanted to die, but there was something else she felt. Something she hadn't experienced in a very long time—unconditional love.

CHAPTER 12

Rehab

Brenda heard the conversations erupting around her. "What do you mean there is nothing you can do?" she heard Josh howl out over the beeping of a machine. There was a mechanical coolness in the response that followed: "Seizures and comas are unfortunately part of the detox process."

"We are doing our best for her. She is strong. She is a fighter," he continued.

"So, this is something she'll pull through, right?" Sheryl asked more for Josh's benefit than her own.

"The medicine we gave her is helping, but now it is up to fate what happens now." He paused. "She has some pre-existing medical conditions, such as diabetes," the doctor said cautiously.

Brenda's heart beat wildly inside of her chest, and for a moment she thought the others could hear it. Was she going to die? She had always wanted to die after losing her children. But was she ready for it to happen? She began to panic but was afraid to show that she was awake. She didn't know if she was prepared to face what awaited her.

"Listen Dr. Alberstein, I understand all of that. Please understand this. If Brenda dies, I'll have your job and everyone who calls themselves a medical professional in this place. I hope you understand that as well."

Brenda's heart stopped, and her panic dissipated as she heard Josh's hard-hitting response.

She heard Sheryl gasp at her husband's retort. "Joshua Lyles, that's enough," Sheryl said sternly.

"Mr. Lyles, I don't take too kindly to threats, and yours is misplaced. We are doing our best to ensure Brenda pulls through this, but you have to understand. Some things are out of even a doctor's control."

"I would have you know, Dr. Alberstein, that I don't make idle threats." And with that, she could hear Sheryl gasp again and someone storm out of the room. She could hear heavy footsteps violently assaulting the ground and assumed they belonged to Josh.

"Dr. Alberstein, please forgive my husband." Brenda could now hear the emotion in Sheryl's throat. "Brenda is one of the only family members Josh has left, and he loves her very much. They have had a rough relationship, but he'll do anything for her. Please forgive him."

Brenda's ears rang in sweet melody at the sound of Sheryl's plea to Dr. Albers… or whoever he was. She couldn't believe what Josh had said, and thought she had never felt so cared for in all her life. Brenda could feel the tears wetting her cheeks as the conversation continued around her. She was too nervous to wipe her eyes or open them. She wanted them to think she was still unconscious.

"Mrs. Lyles, I understand, and I don't hold it against your husband. But I am not a god. I'm just a doctor."

Exhaling loudly, Sheryl responded with a tone of sympathy, "No, Dr. Alberstein, you are not God. But there is a God who does not see this situation the same way you do, or any of us, for that matter. His ways are not our ways and His thoughts are certainly not ours. He will pull Brenda through this. You just wait and see. He has a plan for her life, and he won't allow death to have her before she fulfills it. I will see you tomorrow, Doctor." And with that, Brenda could hear them both leave the room, one after the other.

Laying there, she allowed herself to relax once more, even with throbbing bones. Smiling, she tried to envision things turning around for her.

* * *

Brenda awakened, the chill from the room enveloping her body. She looked around in a daze. No one was there, and she tried to sit up, but her arms felt like spaghetti. With strength zapped from her, she decided to wait a while. Maybe someone would come to check on her soon.

Her last memory was the fight between the doctor and Josh and the conversations she overheard. Pulsing her fingers in and out of a fist, she tried to get her muscles to remember she was still alive. It took effort, but the more she worked them, the more strength she felt. Eventually, she was able to move her arms slowly. She attempted to pull them to her shoulders. She continued until she regained mobility. She sat up as a cramp licked up her back. She gasped slightly and continued her effort.

Brenda heard footsteps hastening towards her room, and she sat up a little straighter against the metal frame. "Ms. Lyles, You're up! Here let me help," the towering female staff member said.

"How long have I been out?"

"I'm Toya, a resident staff member here. And a little under two weeks' ma'am. I'll grab Dr. Alberstein for you and get you up and going," she said brightly as she helped Brenda sit up more comfortably in bed.

"How are you feeling? You got yourself up which is great." Brenda smelled the menthol on Toya's breath and self-consciously put her hand over her mouth. Had her teeth been brushed at all?

"Yes, I got myself up a bit. It was a challenge for sure," Brenda replied. "Can you tell me what the coming days will look like?"

"Well, you will start with counseling sessions. That's thirty days. Then, there is a schedule for you each day that will consist of the Twelve-Step program and other support group sessions." Toya glanced to the stand beside the bed, and Brenda's eyes followed and saw a pamphlet. "There are some other activities listed there that you will be able to participate in," she continued. Brenda tried to take it all in.

"Do you know where they put my things, please? I want to make some calls."

"Umm... actually, it hasn't been a full thirty days yet, Ms. Lyles, so you would need to wait until then before you can start making calls and seeing people other than Mr. and Mrs. Lyles. An exception was made for both of them to come to visit by the director. However, our policy is thirty days." Toya looked behind her at the door and began to back up as she spoke. "I'll get the doctor for you, and he will see you shortly.

Dejected, Brenda relaxed into the bed. She wanted to call Lucky at least. She knew if she did, there would be a big chance she'd be pulled back into the same routine as before. She didn't know if she was strong enough to make it. Images of her children being ripped away from her, along with Sheryl's words, caused determination to swell inside. This had to be it—she needed to make it this time.

* * *

Brenda made it past the program's initial thirty days and felt more alive than she had in years. She breathed deep, allowing fresh air to fill her lungs as she walked through the Renewed Life Rehabilitation Center facility. There was a taste to the fresh air that lingered in her throat. Looking out one of the large windows along the expanse of the hallway, she pressed her hands against the cool glass and looked at the fallen leaves and trees that lined the garden. Gary, Indiana, was more her speed. She enjoyed the slow pace and ability just to be. While this was home, it reminded her of everything she had lost. Josh and Sheryl thought it best for her to be away from the streets of Chicago so that she had fewer temptations to lure her, but close enough for them to visit frequently.

A smile spread as she thought about how Josh and Sheryl looked after her during her treatment. While Josh was overly expressive about how much of an inconvenience she was to his life, she knew that he cared about her more than she had known. Brenda recognized it a few weeks ago when she had a seizure and entered into a coma.

She had completed the detox stage of her rehabilitation journey. She had begun to feel like a normal person again—

whatever that was. She saw the counselor and felt surer than ever before that she wanted to fight for her life.

They cared about each patient completely at this rehabilitation center, she thought. The overall program was more developed than the ones she had experienced in the past. She didn't think she would make it through the detox stage, but she had. She was now in the residential area of the treatment center. She was assigned to attend daily workshops and classes.

Her body still ached for a high. She knew that feeling would probably never go away. Her program was for an entire year, and she had never been clean that long. But how would it be when she was back on the streets having to face reality? She also missed Lucky. She hadn't talked to her friend in over a month. Nevertheless, she wanted this time around to be different.

Brenda gingerly strolled the brightly lit corridor leading to her group counseling session. This may have been a rehabilitation center for people overcoming substance abuse, but it felt more like a fancy hotel with multiple rooms, pleasant food, and exquisite views of the surrounding garden that offered an atmosphere of vivacity. There were scriptures on either side of the hallways and a chapel where a minister came every Sunday to share a word of encouragement with those willing to attend.

Of course, Sheryl would have her admitted to a Christian-based rehabilitation center, Brenda mused. Brenda had been hesitant to think about matters of faith in the past, but her attitude was slowly changing. All she could think about was Sheryl's decree to the doctor that Jesus would save her. It was ironic to her that a non-believing doctor would be working in a Christian rehabilitation center, but Sheryl said it was more common than not.

According to the doctor, patients who got to the state that she was in didn't usually make it out of their coma. Somehow, she had not only made it out of the coma at record-breaking speed, but she had also recovered from the seizure in a way the doctors had never seen before.

"Looking good, Ms. Brenda." Brenda heard a deep baritone voice breaking through the trance of her thoughts. Looking back over her shoulders, she saw Frank removing a bag from the trash bin by the chapel. His smile illuminated the already brightly lit hallway.

Brenda blushed. "Thank you."

"You enjoy your day now," he smiled.

Brenda nodded and continued down the hall. It had been a long time since she had felt like a decent human, let alone pretty or beautiful. Frank was the facility's janitor, or at least that's what she and all the others assumed. He always wore all black and was always cleaning something. Why was he always looking at her so intently? Why was he always smiling? She had to admit he was handsome. Her heart beat wildly as she thought of his smile.

She looked back again over her shoulder. He was staring back at her. Her cheeks flushed, and she quickly jerked her head around and caught her breath. She was a foolish woman. What would make her look back at him so soon? She chided herself for acting like a high school girl. She became self-conscious of her steps, nervous that he was still watching her.

* * *

Brenda sat in the same chair she had sat in the day before. It was a seat where she could see everything, including the door. Taking a survey of the room she saw patients speaking quietly amongst themselves, reading through material, or looking off into the distance, depressed. A woman with dark eyes and pasty skin walked over and took the chair beside her. She must have just taken a shower because her hair was damp and stringy.

"Hey, I'm Laura, I tried to introduce myself yesterday, but you were gone before I made it to you," she said. Brenda was taken aback at the deepness in her voice.

"Hey, I'm Brenda," she said as she shook the woman's sweaty hand.

"I'm 'bout ready for this to be over. My kids made me come, and I don't know how any of this is gonna help." She clung at the purse on her lap that was falling apart at the seams. Brenda forced a smile and hoped the woman wouldn't persist. Her hopes fell short as the woman continued with her complaints. Brenda heard Rene, the class facilitator say, "Hello, let's get started," and she breathed a sigh of relief.

A lanky young guy across the room had some pent-up feelings, and he blurted them out in response to one of the questions asked to the group. "My decisions in life are my decisions. My daughter's only ten. She'll get over it. I been clean for months now. I'm good, and she's good. My journey has nothing to do with anybody else. Who cares what they think?"

His outburst was met with quick gasps and whispers. Some turned to the person sitting next to them, whispering in a not so quiet way. Others shook their heads in disdain.

He shrugged his shoulders and looked at Rene with a confrontational stare. Rene, a heavy-set dark-skinned woman with a southern motherly voice and a tone that demanded respect, responded with a challenging look of her own.

"Desmond, I suggest you be open to learning how to be a better person, not just for your family but for yourself. Remember, the first step is admitting we were powerless over addiction and that our lives became unmanageable. If you want this program to work for you, you'll have to submit to the process like everyone else." Rene looked away and continued as if she was not bothered even a little by Desmond's juvenile attitude.

"Brenda, would you like to share about the people that have been affected by your addiction and those you would like to seek forgiveness from?" Brenda knew the question would come around to her, but it was still salt on an open wound. She swallowed hard as she glanced around at all the gawking faces. Some intent on hearing her response, others with eyes of understanding, and others with arms folded and tapping toes. Laura shifted in her seat. Brenda felt her stomach twisting and beads of sweat on her forehead.

"Uh, well…." She swallowed the air that seemed to choke her. "My addiction has destroyed everything. It has taken everything from me." Someone passed the tissue box her way, but she refused it. "My...my children," she cleared her throat. "My children were taken from me some years back. I have four children, Kendrick, Karissa, Sarah, and Caleb." She could barely get their names out. Her heart beat riotously, but she was determined to say each name. What had holding it in all these years gotten her?

"They were placed in foster care after I left them in a shelter for weeks," she continued, allowing the tears to flow relentlessly. "I asked someone to look out for them, and I..." the woman on the other side of her gave her the tissue, and she took it this time. "I thought they would be fine. They were not. I was not…nothing was fine." Rene gave her a slow and sympathetic nod.

"I don't even know where they are." She blew her nose. At that moment, she was startled by Laura attempting to give her a hug from the side. She wanted to resist but didn't want to embarrass the woman in front of the class.

"I'm fine, thank you," she said instead. "I would say they were most affected by my addiction. They are the ones I would like to seek forgiveness from someday." Brenda pursed her lips together and looked down at her clasped hands. She heard the accustomed "Thank you for sharing, Brenda," and her shoulders loosened.

Heading back to her room, Brenda caught a glimpse of herself through the reflection that swept over the double doors to one of the cafés. It was busy with visitors and patients. She had regained her soft brown skin color, the life returned to her once limp curls that lay effortlessly over her shoulders now, and she had begun to put on weight. Her now curvy hips were proportional with the rest of her body. Brenda smiled and was met with the stains of her past decisions, but she noticed that her teeth looked brighter now. She had forgotten her dimples were one of her favorite features—she hadn't smiled much in a long time.

Brenda had tried to sober up before, but she had never come this far. That didn't mean she didn't yearn for a high every moment of every day. The desire to feel pure ecstasy was the taste in the back of her mouth. However, she had never before felt like she could overcome that feeling until now.

Yes, she had thought she could beat her addiction on her own in the past. Back in her "golden days," as Lucky called them. That was before she found out she was pregnant with her fourth child, Caleb. She remembered the moment with a cold chill in the pit of her stomach. She remembered bursting through Angie's door and falling into her arms. She broke the news that she had been doing drugs and was now going to have another child that would be affected by them. She had seen the effect that crack cocaine and heroin had on some of the kids in her neighborhood. She couldn't believe she would bring a child into the world who would battle life the same way those kids were.

Her young body shook in Angie's arms as the woman who had become a mom to her softly brushed the tears from her cheeks, smoothing the distressed hair back from Brenda's face. "We will pray, Brenda. God will come through for this baby. It will be a miracle. You just wait and see."

"But you have to stop this, Brenda. You have three young kids who need you. I'm not their mother. I can't raise them like they need to be raised."

Angie would always say, "I know who to call on; that's the only one that can do somethin' 'bout anything." Brenda prayed as well. They asked that God protect and prevent her unborn child from developing any developmental defects resulting from her heroin use. She had a relationship with God back then, just not like Angie's. She wasn't strong like Angie and often did things she didn't want to do. Brenda vowed to Angie that day that she would not use heroin again.

That promise lasted about a week. Brenda struggled with drugs throughout the pregnancy. However, the miracle that they prayed for came in the way of Caleb's apparent ability to fight all the assumed symptoms of the drug. Brenda remembered wanting to serve the Lord with all her heart at that point. But the addiction waged war against her and eventually smothered the desire for God altogether.

CHAPTER 13

The unexpected

"Karissa, just come to the game night. It'll be fun." Sariah's voice resonated from the other end of the phone.

"Sariah, I'm not interested in being around a lot of people right now. I've had a long week. I honestly need to rest. I don't feel like leaving my apartment right now."

The truth that both Karissa and Sariah knew was that Karissa didn't want to be around Sariah's "church friends." The last group outing she attended didn't end so well. The conversation veered into the topic of homosexuality and sexual sin in the world, and Karissa chimed in with her take on their "judgmental comments."

"You know they don't like me anyway. I don't know why you keep inviting me to their stuff," Karissa said matter-of-factly.

Sariah laughed, "Karissa, nobody ever told you that. You just think everyone is trying to judge you all the time. You ran out last time for no reason. You know you can just say when you disagree without leaving all the time. Just chill and be a part of the conversation. Those people have their own business to mind. Trust me, they're not sitting around judging you."

"Umm-hmm," was all Karissa added.

She had to admit it to herself. She was a runner for sure—something Sariah pointed out to her back in their Brookdale University days.

"Karissa, I have known you for years. Right now, you're in your sweatpants, sitting on the couch, eating a spoon of peanut butter, and watching reruns of *Scandal.* You need to get out of the house, is all I am saying. Isolating yourself is depressing."

Karissa dropped the spoon of peanut butter back in the jar. She looked over at the TV screen, which was paused on a scene where Olivia Pope was trying to crack a case with her Gladiators. She shook her head at the phone and was both amused and annoyed that Sariah knew her so well.

"Fine Sariah, but the moment they say something stupid, I'm out," Karissa emphasized in a sharp tone.

She could almost hear Sariah's smile through the phone. "OK, awesome! I'll text you the details," and with that, Karissa flopped face down on her couch. She didn't know why she always let Sariah get her way.

Her face was buried in the cushion of her couch, so she turned her head to face the TV. She reached behind her to grab the remote that was under her thigh. She hit the play button and let the remote drop between her fingers to the carpeted floor.

On the screen, Olivia skillfully lined photos up on the wall as she spoke to her team about potential suspects. Karissa loved Olivia's confidence and boldness. She felt she could relate to the way Olivia lived her life in this drama series. Karissa knew she was seen as beautiful and strong by others, just like Olivia. Karissa was also very confident, or at least that's how she was perceived. The only difference between how she saw Olivia Pope versus herself was that she felt lost inside. It was something she could never pinpoint, and didn't know how to express.

To be honest, nothing in all her life scared her more than the vulnerable feeling of not knowing who she was and feeling that something was strangely missing. She picked up her phone and did the one thing she always did when she felt depressed—look for the attention that would distract her from the annoying feelings welling up inside of her.

She scrolled through her contacts and landed on Steve's name. A sly smile inched its way across her lips. Steve was a guy she had been talking with for a couple of years now. He was a Brooklyn guy. He had the type of swag and smooth words that made her skin hot all over and caused her to blush when he was around. He was tall with the smoothest chocolate skin and deep brown eyes.

Her heart abruptly skipped a beat as Nate flashed through her mind. She rolled her eyes at herself and began to type the message to Steve, rebelling against the feelings of loyalty to Nate.

Why did he have to come to mind, he was not her man, and she had moved on from that season of her life. Besides, she was sure Nate was celibate, or "pure," or whatever they called it. He would see her as someone who would taint him, and she could not bear the thought of him thinking about her that way.

She hadn't talked to Steve since she ran into Nate over a month ago at Rachel's "co-worker's" birthday celebration. Karissa never took Steve too seriously, although he wanted her to. He was one of those guys that all the women drooled over and even threw themselves at shamelessly. Karissa, on the other hand, was not the least bit desperate for any man. She met Steve at a happy hour event she and a few co-workers attended right before Valentine's Day. She decided to go out with some co-workers since they, too, were single and didn't have dates planned.

She made sure she was dressed to turn heads that night. She wore her form-fitted red dress with black stiletto pumps. She loved the days she felt like dressing up. She was mostly a fan of natural beauty, but every so often, she loved to show off a little. When she and her co-workers Rebecca and Shana arrived, they could feel the atmosphere's magnetic liveliness. There were people all over; it was a private event hosted by a colleague of theirs.

Rebecca, the outspoken one who had the most gorgeous blond hair and green eyes she had ever seen, motioned for them to follow her. They moved toward the back to find decent standing space. Karissa sauntered towards the back in her usual self-assured but focused way, and that's when she spotted Steve. Her heart dropped instantly as butterflies danced wildly in her belly. He charmed her with a beautiful smile.

He was dark as the shirt he wore underneath his tailored cream blazer, which caused him to stand out even more in the room. She saw there were women all around him covertly fighting for his attention with overly obnoxious laughs and flirty arm grabbing.

His eyes pierced through her, seemingly ignoring the attention. She smiled, embarrassed as Shana looked over her shoulder at Karissa, clearly aware of the interaction. Shana winked at her and mouthed, "OMG, yes, girl, he's cute." She could hear it in her head just the way Shana would say it, and she laughed.

When Karissa looked back at the ravishing chocolate dream of a man, his spellbinding gaze caught hers once more. Steve was the type of guy that could charm his way into any place he wanted—even her heart. She knew that she couldn't let that happen.

He had begun to tell her he wanted things to go to the next level, but Karissa knew he didn't have a faithful bone in his body. She loved the attention, and she loved their nights together, but wasn't foolish enough to fall for him. She would enjoy him in the way she wanted, but she wouldn't allow herself to be a fool like the other women.

Sariah and Rachel didn't know about Steve. He was Karissa's guilty pleasure, and she didn't want that spoiled by their judgmental thinking. They assumed she wasn't talking to anyone at the moment.

There were a lot of things they didn't know about her. She preferred to keep some things away from them. She didn't want them worrying or lecturing. They may have had different ways of showing their concern for her, but Karissa felt sometimes caged by both approaches.

They didn't know that Karissa had two abortions over the past three years. One from Steve and another from someone she could barely remember. She was not proud of her decisions, and she didn't want her friends looking at her differently because of it.

Karissa placed her hands over her belly as the memories flooded her mind. She sometimes wondered what her children would be like—how they would look. Her eyes burned as she felt the sting of guilt and regret engulf her already vexed emotions.

She shoved the thoughts from her mind and began to form her text to Steve. "Hey, you. What are you up to?" She stared at the phone, waiting. Did she really want to do this? Uneasiness crept in.

Her phone dinged as his response popped up. "Hey, you! Got some business to take care of, but after that, I'm free. Want to link up?"

She promised Sariah that she would come to her friends' gathering this evening. Still, she wanted to hang out with Steve. It was three-thirty on a Saturday afternoon, so she could link up with Steve first and then head to Sariah's gathering.

Thinking over the details before she responded, Karissa calculated the risk. She hated talking to Sariah after engaging in "sin." Not that she thought Sariah would judge her if she did know, but she just didn't feel comfortable around her after "playing the harlot." It was like she felt unclean, and that got under her skin.

Rolling her eyes, Karissa rebelliously responded to Steve's message. "Where do you want to meet?"

After solidifying their plans, she decided to take a quick nap before heading out for the night. She stretched out on the couch and pulled her blanket over herself, and drifted into oblivion.

Karissa panted heavily as she ran through the familiar house. There was a sense of darkness that closed around and caused a panic that felt like death. Fear closed in around her. "Please help me, help me please," she heard a child's voice beckoning her with a piercing cry.

Running with all her might, Karissa ignored the darkness as if she was nocturnal. As she ran, lights began to flicker off and on as if she was in a haunted house. It was the same house she had visited many times before, but this time it felt more haunted. It was like there was a dark presence lurking around her.

She saw the door in the flickering light, and she grabbed at the knob, using all of her strength to open the door. This time it wouldn't open. She pulled, kicked, and pulled again with no progress, tears flowing down her face. She heard the child screaming, and she banged on the door with her fist dropping to the ground with a rush of defeat that left her breathless.

"I'm sorry," she bellowed through her sobs. She had never felt so defeated. "I'm sorry, I can't get to you," she yelled, this time hoarser than before.

She then felt a jarring kick on the other side of the door like an invisible force threatening to burst through. She fell backward then immediately scrambled to her feet just as the door flew open.

Karissa woke up, panting frantically. She felt the dark presence still surrounding her. She leaped up from the couch with sweat covering her face and back. She tried to catch her breath. Fear gripped her. Looking around the apartment, still hazy from the dream, she bent over, trying to ease the panic inside of her. "Breathe in, breathe out, Karissa. Breathe," she coached herself as her hands gripped her thighs.

Drawing herself up, she flopped down on the couch again, closing her eyes, focusing on her breathing. Tears began to well up. What was wrong with her? Was she going crazy after all? Why had this dream become so persistent lately? What was happening to her? Each time she had this dream, it became more frightening, more intense. She had to find out what was happening to her.

She thought of Amanda, and frustration washed over her. She had a feeling that she should have stuck it out, but her pride wouldn't let her admit it openly. She knew that something had been out of kilter with her for a while now. It wasn't like she wasn't aware of the emptiness spreading through her existence. She had enough self-awareness to understand that. But she couldn't give voice to it. Sariah was just a call away. She could easily talk to her about it, but her friend wouldn't allow her to go at her own pace. She knew if she told Sariah she secretly wanted help, that Sariah would begin to call her pastors, leaders, parents, and everyone else she could. She didn't want it to become a big deal. Everyone had problems, right?

* * *

Karissa got into her SUV and drove across the Manhattan Bridge to meet Steve at one of her favorite places, which was on Lafayette near Third Street in Manhattan. She walked through the doors of Seafood Bar and Grill at 6:30 in the evening. The ambiance was just how she liked it, dimmed lighting that etched romance in her veins and stunning chandeliers hanging from snow white ceilings.

She looked around trying to spot Steve, when she caught a glimpse of herself in the mirror. She wore her new knee-length peacoat with puffed sleeves, along with her red dress that fit her curves like a glove. She wore black pumps with the matching black chained purse that hung over her shoulder. She fluffed her curls to add more volume and smiled to make sure her lipstick hadn't stained her teeth.

A group of couples walked past her, but she continued to check herself out in the full-length mirror at the entrance. When she finished sizing herself up, Karissa turned to walk into the restaurant's seated area.

A group of guys walked past the host station giving very lively greetings. Karissa didn't want to be bothered by their attention, so she stopped in her tracks and pretended to look for something in her purse.

The group of exiting men slowed at the sight of her. She saw only their crisp expensive shoes because she refused to look up.

"Wow, my god," one remarked in a low husky voice.

Karissa pretended not to notice them. Other men also slowed, but they continued past her, making shrewd remarks as they did. A brave one wouldn't move on, and she looked up and peered at him through narrow eyes.

"May I help you?" she asked coolly, her words caught in her throat. She glanced coldly at the group of men, and her heart nearly stopped when she saw the man standing behind the cocky short guy. She stumbled back as the eyes of the tall man held hers boldly, unrelentingly.

"N-Na-Nate, what are you doing here?" was all she could get out. Her heart beat as if her life was on the line, and her brain could not catch up to where she was or what was happening. It felt as if the room was closing in around her, and all that was alive and active was Nate. His big audacious eyes leaped through the barriers of her soul and refused to retreat. His hands were in his coat pockets, and he was cemented in place.

"Karissa." He let her name settle on his lips. He looked her over and paused again before he spoke. "You...you're breathtaking."

"Thank you." She stumbled over her words as she looked at him through shocked eyes and a deep love, she knew she would never feel for any other man.

"Why have you been running from me, Karissa?" he asked as he began to walk closer to her closing the gap between them.

Karissa slowly backed away from him. “I’m not running from you. We haven’t spoken in years. We’re just in different places, is all.” She backed herself against the wall and had no more space to add between them.

“It doesn’t matter. I wanted to marry you then. And I’ve never wanted another woman since.” This time he was face-to-face with her with no more than an inch separating them. His hand came to her face.

Karissa could not believe what he had just said or the look in his eyes as he said it. Her heart could not take it. She glanced past him and saw his pack of friends grinning at them as they whispered to one another. Then she measured the distance between her and the exit.

He took strands of her hair and rubbed them between his fingers, drinking in the sight of her. “You may not be ready right now…” he looked deep into her eyes, “Just know that I love you, and I never gave up. On you, or us.”

Karissa closed her eyes tightly, trying to block the impact of his words. She felt his body draw near to hers, and before she could open her eyes, his lips were on hers—gentle and smooth. She wanted to pull back but could not. She melted into him as if they had never spent a day without each other. He drew back first, looking down at her as if he carried her in his heart all his life.

"I'm sorry," Nate said, clearly conflicted. She could tell he wrestled and knew why.

Karissa cringed at his words. She had come to the restaurant with the intent to leave with Steve, and here Nate was apologizing for kissing her. Shame washed over her, and she snapped out of the moment.

"Listen, Nate, if you want to know the truth, here it is. I love you. I never stopped loving you. I don't think I ever could. But we are different. Too different." Nate could see distress and distance in Karissa's eyes.

She then turned away from him and ran out of the restaurant, forgetting why she had gone there in the first place. She looked over her shoulder when she made it to her car. Nate was standing in the same spot where she left him. He was mouthing words, and she knew he was praying. Her heart stopped when she saw him wiping tears from his eyes. What manner of love was this that he would cry for her? She almost broke at the sight of it. Instead, she jumped into her SUV and sped off.

"Steve. Crap," Karissa yelled out as she sped up the street. She stopped abruptly at a stop sign she almost missed. Pedestrians spilled into the street. She swore and hit the steering wheel. She reached into her pocket for her phone. She kept her foot on the brake and let them all cross.

Steve, I'm so sorry. Something came up, and I won't be able to make it today. I'm sorry to keep you waiting..." She would send this part to get a message through immediately then finish the message when she made it home.

Her stomach kicked wildly with wonder as she felt Nate's mouth on hers and the longing in his eyes. What did he want from her? She was not going to become someone other than who she was for him. He wanted more than she could give. Her head began to pound as she fought to shake Nate from her mind.

She glanced in her rear-view mirror as she drove, as if Nate or Steve might be following her. She caught a glimpse of herself in the mirror. She was a wreck, she cringed inwardly. Not on the outside—her makeup was still flawless. Her hair lay voluptuously around her face and over her shoulders, and the new skincare regime made her skin look velvety smooth.

It was the look in her own eyes that frightened her. The look of vacancy sent a chill through her. She saw through to her soul and felt more lost than ever before. Who was she, and what was she doing? She looked back at her phone and saw the bubbled dots letting her know that Steve was responding. Her heart raced. She would go home to process all that had happened and tell him she would come over later. She pulled back on the road, more determined than ever to get home.

* * *

Karissa's eyes jolted up when she heard a loud, ear-piercing horn and screeching. Her life flashed before her eyes as a pickup truck was coming right at her from the intersection she was crossing. She realized the light had turned red; she was distracted when she gazed into the mirror. Her heart leaped out of her chest as she tried to hysterically turn the car in the opposite direction. "Oh God, no!" were the last words she spoke before the truck crashed violently into her passenger side.

Her car went crashing into another vehicle that could not avoid the impending accident. Then her SUV brutally flipped multiple times before she lost consciousness. Karissa's last thought was if this was her last day, how had her life mattered? She braced herself for death.

CHAPTER 14

Panic

"I said I won't do it again. If you don't believe me, then whatever." Emma rolled her eyes as she fidgeted in her seat, ready to go. Sariah ignored the comment from the stubborn girl whom she had mentored for almost five years.

"Em, this is me you're talking to. Hello…" Sariah said with riveted attention, waving her hand to show that she was in front of Emma and not out the window where she stared absently. Emma jolted her head in Sariah's direction with a challenging look.

Sariah continued, "How many times am I going to have to take you to the clinic for the same issues? You want to catch something that can't be cured?" *Lord, she gives her body away as if she hates her own soul.* Sariah's heart ached.

"I don't care! I never asked you to take me nowhere. That's yo' choice, not mine," Emma retorted. The young girl rolled her eyes and folded her arms across her chest. While Sariah's small work office was not quite the cozy temperature needed for a December day in Brooklyn, she knew Em wasn't fighting an external chill.

Sariah's eyes flashed, and she wanted to shake the girl. She felt deflated. Her mind flickered to Karissa. Had she ever been able even to reach her friend? Her eyes moistened, and she lowered her head as guilt washed over her. *Be still and know that I am God* resounded within her, and she knew the Lord was speaking. It wasn't by her strength and ability that she would see anyone turn to Jesus or become who He created them to be. It would be the Lord's doing. She warmed and turned her attention back to Emma with renewed hope.

"Look, Em, I know you're trying to push me away. But guess what? I'm not going anywhere. So, I guess you're stuck with me, and you're gonna have to learn to live with it," Sariah said more lightly. She saw Em soften and relax a bit. "I know you've had a hard life. You're only sixteen, and you've been through more than people who are twice your age. But you know what?" Emma shrugged nonchalantly.

Sariah continued, "The day I was assigned to mentor you, I knew you were special. I told them that no matter what, I wanted to stick with you until you aged out of the Raise Them Up program. And beyond…." Sariah spoke passionately, wanting her love to pierce Emma's hardness. Sariah was grateful she brought Emma back to her office while she finished up an assignment. It was the weekend, and no one was there, so she could talk freely with her.

"Ms. Blake, you was there fa' me when I had my abortions and when I was in juvey and everything. But you not me. You don't get it. You don't know what it's like to know my parents didn't want me, and my grandma is just tolerating me. You don't know nothing," Emma said in her New York accent. Tears freely flowed down Emma's yellow cheeks and Sariah's heart broke.

She rushed to her, kneeling. "Look at me Em. I don't know. You're right. I don't know what bothers you inside, and I don't know your personal pain." Emma used her sleeve to forcefully wipe her tears. Sariah continued, "But you want to know something I haven't shared with anybody, not even my closest friends?" She saw that she now had Emma's full attention.

Sariah exhaled. Closing her eyes, she prayed for help.

"I used to get molested by a very close family member for years when I was a little girl." Sariah's eyes welled.

"Fa'real?" Emma asked with wide-eyed disbelief.

"Yes. In my own house with someone I loved and trusted more than anything." She let the tears fall. "I thought I deserved it. For so long I thought it was my fault. That I deserved what he did to me." She allowed the tormented memories to flood back in. Emma reached for Sariah's hands and crossed them in hers.

"People look at my life now and think I don't know suffering. But I do Em. I understand when life isn't fair and the people you love and trust the most betray you, hurt you, disappoint you sometimes…."

Sariah wiped her tears and looked deeply into Emma's eyes. But before she could continue, Em broke in. "Why you never told nobody?" Her question was sincere.

Sariah paused and let the reality sink in. Fresh tears came. "I was afraid at first. I thought if I said something, no one would believe me. I thought that maybe I had done something to deserve it. And I thought if my family was destroyed by me saying something, it would be my fault," Sariah sighed. "Later in life, I guess I thought it didn't matter anymore. I have forgiven the person and love them very much. So, I thought it would be best not to expose them."

Emma got up and grabbed a tissue from a box on Sariah's desk. She handed it to Sariah and got down on her knees face-to-face with her. Emma wrapped her arms around Sariah, holding onto her tightly. She cried and Sariah knew that it was her she cried for now.

Pulling herself together, Sariah pulled away and got up, and helped Emma up. They both sat back down, and Sariah pulled her chair closer. She paused and allowed her heart to settle.

The reality was that she could not reach Emma at the place of her pain and suffering because she refused to acknowledge her own pain. Her mind flickered to Karissa. Would she have been able to reach her friend if she only opened up about her own dark past? *My grace is enough for you. My strength is made perfect in your weakness.* The Holy Spirit's gentle reminder filled her. She looked up and smiled into Emma's now softened countenance.

"Ms. Blake, you the bubbliest person I know. It's like you wake up to rainbows and sunshine every day. How you like that with what you been through?"

"One thing I can tell you that I do know beyond a shadow of a doubt, Em. That is the only reason I was able to overcome is because of Jesus. I don't want to sound cliché, but it's the honest truth." Her eyes rested on Emma. "I wouldn't be here today if it wasn't for Him. I wouldn't have been able to forgive my father if it wasn't for Him. I…" Emma's eyes flashed in shock and pain.

Sariah stopped in her tracks, realizing what she had just done. She closed her eyes and scolded herself inwardly. "Yes, it was my father." She paused to let that sink in. "But I have forgiven him, Em. I hated him for a long time. I hated *myself* for a long time. It was the Lord who met me in my pain and loved me out of it. It was Jesus who set me free from shame and unforgiveness. That's what He can do for you too, Em."

“I think I would like that Ms. Blake,” Em said as a light shone from her eyes.

* * *

After Sariah dropped Emma off, she pulled her phone out of her bag for the first time that day. And what a day it had been. It was a Saturday, and these were the days she met with Emma. Sometimes they went out, or somedays they met at her workspace. She was exhausted beyond words and knew she had to muster up the strength to hang out with Brandon later. She promised him that she would go ax-throwing with him. Of all things! She had no interest in doing such a thing and saw no fun in it. Why didn’t he want to go ice skating or to the aquarium or anything but ax-throwing?

Looking through her phone while keeping one eye on the road, she saw several texts from Brandon, a missed call from her mom, and a message from Rachel that read “URGENT.” Looking through her rearview mirror, a taxicab was riding her tail. Sariah tried to focus. What in the world could be an urgent situation coming from Rachel? It had to be about Karissa. Her heart dropped. Ignoring all other calls and messages, she swiped the message opening it to see again. What could it be? She thought to herself impatiently.

“Hey Siri, call Rachel.” As Rachel’s number rang through the speaker, Sariah contemplated the possibilities.

"Sariah! Girl, where have you been?" Rachel yelled from the other end of the phone. Sariah heard the panic in her voice and knew immediately that something was tragically wrong. She pulled her car over, trying not to get run off the road by intolerant New York drivers.

"Rachel, what is it?" Sariah asked in a forced, controlled tone.

"OK…" breathing in and out heavily, Rachel tried to calm down. "Karissa…" Rachel began to cry, and Sariah felt her heart leap out of her chest.

"Rachel, what happened to Karissa? You have to calm down and tell me what happened." Cars screeched past her, and she turned off the speaker and put the phone to her ear.

"Ka-Karissa was in…" sobs echoed, "… a really bad car accident, and they don't think she will make it." Rachel began to cry hysterically.

Sariah felt her own life flash before her eyes and began to break down herself. "Oh my God, no. Jesus, please no." Sariah tried to be the calm one since Rachel was falling apart, but she couldn't think straight as fear darkened everything around her.

"They…they… are saying she has internal bleeding. Sariah, I don't know what to do," Rachel said in a breathy whisper. "They need someone who is family to communicate with. She's in a coma and will not likely come out of it is all they could tell me." Rachel paused, trying to control her sobs. "My number was the last one in her phone. They shared more information with me than they were supposed to, the officer said."

Sariah couldn't hear anything past "*they don't think she's going to make it.*"

"You know I'm not into this God thing, but please pray right now. I can't imagine losing her, Sariah." That request jolted Sariah out of her trance, like a bucket of ice water to the face. "You're right, Rachel," wiping her tears in an attempt to regain control. "Let's pray, but what hospital is she at? I'll head there now."

* * *

Sariah strode purposefully through the NYU Community Hospital that was located near the scene of the accident. She didn't like hospitals because they depressed her. Braving the turbulent wave of panic, she silently prayed asking God to give her courage and peace. She couldn't think about herself right now, she needed all of her energy to be present for Karissa.

Briskly bypassing the emergency room waiting area, the smell of the hospital assaulted her senses, leaving her head swimming with nausea. The piercing sounds of babies crying, and loud conversations grated, and she almost forgot why she was there. Her head began to throb as she approached the front desk. There were three women behind the desk who all seemed to be too preoccupied to notice her. There was a guy a few inches shorter than her with a baseball cap on, shifting from one foot to the other, clearly growing increasingly impatient. He was next in line behind a woman with two toddlers hanging onto her legs.

"Mommy, I'm hungry," cried the little girl with the pink jacket and clutching a doll. Her mother patted her head and bent down to whisper something to her before finishing her conversation with the receptionist.

When it was finally Sariah's turn, she approached the heavy-set woman, who was finishing up work on her computer.

"How can I help you," she said flatly, pushing her glasses up with her finger.

"I am here to see a friend. Her name is Karissa Sparks." Sariah's voice broke, and she saw the woman soften. She knew the employee was used to seeing hundreds of patients weekly, if not daily. She probably learned not to let her emotions consume her. Her stoic face gently relaxed as she began typing something on her computer.

"Are you family?"

"I'm like her sister. I'm the closest person to her here in New York." Sariah grew more panic-stricken as she unbuttoned her jacket and smoothed her curls back from her face.

She saw the woman look back to her computer with a confused look. *Lord, please help. Please let Karissa live.*

"I'm sorry, but we are not allowed to disclose any information unless to a family member," the woman said to her unwaveringly.

Sariah's tears began to spill over as she put her hand to her mouth. *Father, what am I to do? Please give me wisdom.*

Her phone began to ring, "I'm sorry I have to answer this," she told the woman. Seeing Rachel's name pop up on the screen she felt a sense of relief.

"Rachel," Sariah said quickly. "I'm pulling up now, about to park. Are you inside?"

"Yes, I am. Please hurry. They won't let me see her, and they won't release any information."

"Ma'am, I'm going to need you to step aside, please," the woman said, trying to hide her impatience.

Sariah looked up and saw no one else behind her and wondered why the woman needed her to get out of line. She decided not to fuss and walked off.

Sariah stood near the vending machine by the emergency room entrance and saw Rachel jogging in her direction. Sariah noticed how radiant Rachel looked with her long braids and athletic wear. It looked like she was coming from the gym. Sariah always thought Rachel could have a career as a bodybuilder if she wanted one. Her defined muscular build always stood out, along with her smooth dark skin.

"Rachel," exclaimed Sariah. They clung to each other more out of comfort than anything else. Sariah knew Rachel despised her faith and maybe even her—but she loved Rachel and admired her loyalty to Karissa. While Karissa never had a problem with holding her own, Rachel was a fierce protector and always there. She didn't always agree with Rachel's ways, but she tried her best never to judge her.

"Rachel, I don't know what to do," Sariah whispered brokenly. "Let me take care of it. Stay here, and I'll come for you," Rachel said in a take-charge way. In the many encounters she had with her, she was always loud and boisterously joking or sharing some dramatic perspective on some issue. But she trusted that Rachel would do whatever it took to get the information concerning Karissa.

Sariah knew that Rachel was up to something by the mischievous wink she gave as she looked over her shoulder from the front desk. Rachel paced in front of the desk, anxiously passing the time. She almost knocked a kid over as the child ran away from his father, who was chasing after him. Rachel looked sternly at the dark-headed, wide-eyed boy as the father caught up to him red with embarrassment.

I know you have a plan and purpose for Rachel, Lord. She's stubborn as Karissa but even more set in her ways. I pray for her salvation. Allow her to encounter you in a way that would make her a believer. You did it so many times in the scriptures, Lord. You showed your nail-pierced hands to Thomas when he doubted you. You were transfigured in front of Peter, James, and John. And you worked countless miracles that caused people to believe. And when I wanted to take my life when I was twelve? I took the whole bottle of ibuprofen eight hundred and woke up the next day with nothing but a headache. Would you show up the same for Rachel? And would you use this accident to draw Karissa into a relationship with you? Do the impossible, Lord. Sariah felt a breeze wash over her, and she knew the Lord was there. He was always there, and she loved talking to Him as she would a friend.

Sariah noted that it was a different woman talking to Rachel, not the one she spoke with. That woman was on the phone while simultaneously typing at her computer.

Smelling the scent of coffee, Sariah tried to locate it. She looked down the hall to the left and saw the coffee station with a few people surrounding it. As she got up and headed towards it when her phone rang.

It was Rachel reporting in from across the room. "Rachel, what happened," Sariah asked, pausing in her tracks.

"They gave me the information for Karissa. I'm going back to speak with the doctor. I'll be back." With that, Rachel hung the phone up and followed a Hispanic woman with long wavy hair into the depths of the hospital.

Sariah was stunned and wondered what Rachel had done that she hadn't. She decided to reject thoughts of comparison and took a chair across the room. She tried to block out the noise, the lighting that made it hard to rest her eyes, and the smell of sickness and disease.

Just as she began to relax her eyes, they jolted open in a realization that sent her scrambling for her phone in her purse. Uncrossing her legs, she arose from her chair, grabbed her bag, and walked towards the coffee maker.

"Hey Siri, call Brandon," she spoke closely to her phone. She was supposed to connect with her boyfriend earlier, but Karissa's accident blotted other thoughts out of her mind.

"Excuse us," an older man said as he walked past her, grabbing the hand of who she assumed was his wife. The hospital was busy with people from all nationalities. Thank God she rarely had reason to be in a hospital, but she couldn't help the way her heart twisted with all the unknown suffering there.

"Hey, baby, what's happening? I've been waiting for your call?" Brandon rasped through the phone, and her heart settled. She picked her medium roast coffee K-cup, grabbed a disposable coffee cup, and plopped the K-cup into the coffee maker.

"Brandon," she said in a tone of relief. "Karissa's been in a terrible accident. I made it to the emergency room not too long ago, and I wasn't able to get any information because I wasn't immediate family," she said dejectedly.

"Karissa? Oh no. What happened?" he responded in a tone drenched in concern.

Just then, two women with head wraps and tunics walked in her direction, eyeing the coffee station. They were speaking in what sounded like Arabic. One was consoling the other with a comforting arm as she wiped away tears.

"Rachel is here, and Lord knows what she said to the front desk staff. They took her back, so prayerfully she will know what's going on soon." Sariah grabbed her coffee from the Keurig and walked back towards the waiting area. She likes her coffee with cream and sugar but decided she needed the strength of the undiluted caffeine.

"I'll come to you as soon as I finish up here. I don't have any plans tonight and am not slated to serve tomorrow at service, so I can stay with you as long as you need me," Brandon said with deep compassion in his voice.

They had been together for a little over a year, and she loved him more and more each day. He knew how much she loved Karissa, and he had grown to love her as well. Karissa and Brandon had not always seen eye to eye, but Brandon saw God's hand on Karissa's life just as much as she had.

"Thank you, baby, but let me find out what's going on before you come here."

They ended the call, and Sariah got up and paced the floor. Five minutes later, she saw Rachel coming from the double doors leading into the waiting room. The look on her face sent a lick of pain through Sariah's heart, and she knew that whatever it was, they would need a miracle from God.

CHAPTER 15

The Encounter

Karissa's eyes fluttered erratically. She could feel the officer's hands trying to extract her from her SUV, but she felt life slipping from her. The pain was vicious, and she could taste death as blood poured from her. She tried to speak but couldn't. Her heart slowed, her breath became shallow, and she plummeted into oblivion.

And then there was light.

Where am I? Karissa thought. She couldn't make out her surroundings.

She was overcome with peace, and light seemed to radiate through her being. Intoxicating scents of sweetness she had never smelled nearly caused her to laugh out loud. Where was she? She tried to focus her gaze but couldn't make out the figures before her. It seemed there was a veil of some sort over her eyes. She didn't move, afraid she would walk into a wall. She rubbed frantically at her eyes but couldn't seem to escape the sheer film that blurred her vision.

"Hello," she tried to yell, but no sound came out. Her heart beat wildly as she tried to escape the terror she felt. Through the fog that distorted her vision, she saw things moving past her so fast she couldn't make out what they were. She knew they were not human because she saw something otherworldly on their backs as if they were giant birds. She thought she would die of fear—she was paralyzed in place and couldn't move. She could hear much better than she could see. It sounded like millions of voices in an ocean of unity— "Holy, holy, holy is the Lord God Almighty Who was and is and is to come."

The sound swept through her, and she knew she must be in a dream. Turning her head from left to right, she tried desperately to see what was happening. She saw something too big to measure that looked as if it was on a bigger-than-life high-backed chair. She felt it might have been a throne. Figures hurried in all directions, and it seemed almost as if they were moving through her.

She tried to lift her arms, but they lay stone-like at either side. *Am I dead?* She thought as flashes of being rushed into the hospital flooded her mind. The pain had been so excruciating that she wasn't surprised that she had died. She wished it as they ripped open her blood-stained dress. She hoped that she would just die and be released from her misery.

Karissa began to spin as she lifted off her feet. Her stomach dropped to the floor. She felt as if she was on a roller coaster. She could still not make out where she was, but she felt more relaxed than she had in all her life.

She landed in a strange place, and her vision was more apparent than before. There was still distortion, but she felt that if she had glasses on, she could see clearly. Things looked distant, but she thought they were closer than they appeared. Her head swam with lightness as she heard a voice from behind her. "Karissa." The voice caressed her soul.

She turned swiftly, fear washing over her. It looked like a huge lion. She fell, sure that if she wasn't dead already, fear would definitely kill her. She wanted to run but couldn't. She fell prostrate on what seemed to be a cloud-like surface. The voice was coming from the lion, and it was a voice saturated with power. It was unlike anything she had ever heard before. She wanted to be far away from whatever it was. She had many unusual dreams before, but never anything like this. The thing that shook her to her core was that it felt more real than anything she had ever experienced before. She had never felt more alive than she did right now.

"Don't be afraid, Karissa. I am the first and the last, the Alpha and Omega, the beginning and the end." The voice moved something deep within her. She couldn't comprehend what she was feeling or what she just heard. *Alpha and Omega. Beginning and the end. What?*

She lifted her head slowly, and the speaking lion began walking in her direction, eyes intent on her. It was as if she saw a vision that she couldn't shake herself from, and strangely she was not sure she wanted to shake it off. Fear and awe licked through her body as she tried to back away from the force of power she felt emanating from the beast.

For a moment, her vision cleared, and she looked straight into the eyes of the lion. While the lion's stature exuded an authority that was not like any authority on earth, the look in his eyes was a love she had never known until that moment. A whirlwind seemed to billow, and light shone through it. She trembled and knew wherever she was, and whatever was happening, something was changing deep within her.

He came close to her face, so close she could look into the eyes of the lion and saw a passion of fire. Those eyes didn't look at her, but they looked into her. It was as if nothing was hidden. The mane on the beast was full and striking, and the face had a human quality. Karissa felt her head suddenly become heavy and her body weakened. She was already on the cloud-like surface, so she knew she wouldn't fall far if she fainted. Her eyes became heavy, and she gave way to the abrupt sluggishness in her body and drifted away. Her last memory was the voice of the lion who said, "I release you from your fear."

* * *

Frightened, Karissa ran up the familiar stairs allowing the railing to support her. She refused to look upward to avoid the debilitating fear from keeping her from the task at hand.

Gut-wrenching sobs pierced through the quietness of the house. "I want to go home. I want mommy." The voice of the child tormented her.

She refused to fail this time. She would do whatever it took to make it to the child. Beads of sweat bounced from her brow to her eyes. She blinked quickly, stopping to catch her breath. She gripped the rail tightly and looked up slowly. What she saw took her breath away. She swallowed hard and backed away slowly.

She was in the center of a large empty room with gray walls, which may have been white at some point in the past. There was no furniture, no decorations, and no life. Dust and smells of musk and mildew assaulted her senses. She pulled her hoodie up and adjusted it to cover her nose. Looking left, then right, Karissa saw a figure seated in the corner. All she could see was dark curly hair over pulled-up knees. Her heart broke into millions of pieces as she walked towards the little girl.

"Hi, I'm here to help you," she spoke softly into the deafening silence.

The curly head began to lift. Grief overwhelmed Karissa, and she felt the pain that had long been buried within her. The little girl's dirt-stained face had streaks from the rivulets of tears she had cried.

The little girl had a vacant look in her eyes that ripped Karissa's heart out of her chest. It seemed the little girl was present in body, but fear and abandonment seemed to have smothered the life out of her. She was all alone, and her aloneness spoke louder than the fear. Falling forward with her hands on the filthy ground, Karissa knew the little girl was her, and she wept with an ache she couldn't define.

Darkness pulled her in, and she was disoriented once again. The world was spinning so fast she was nauseous. Looking up, Karissa was no longer in the room with the little girl. The ground dropped beneath her, and she was falling. She tried to yell but she couldn't get any words out. "Please help me," she tried to scream, but the words caught in her throat. She reached and grasped at nothing but air.

What was happening to her, she thought as she lifted her head. She was on the cloud-like surface again. Her eyes danced in wonder as she took in all that was before her. *Was she in heaven?* There was no such place. *Was there?* There was bright color all around her, and peace flooded her body.

She looked down to see what she was lying on, and saw gold stretched out before her. It seemed to have no end. She gingerly ran her hands along the ground, feeling its smoothness and wondering what it was and why she was there.

She heard sounds of laughter behind her, and she cautiously turned her head and saw a man standing and talking freely with a group of people. His back was to her, but she could see they loved him and drank in every word he said.

Men and women of all nationalities joined together, and she felt an otherworldly unity among them.

A group of about ten young people were walking in their direction. They were laughing without a care in the world and playfully jostled one another. "Jesus! Jesus!" exclaimed a girl who was about ten years old. She ran up to the man through the crowd and jumped into his arms. He joyfully picked her up and spun her around. He kissed her on the forehead as he sat her back on her feet. The others stopped, joined the crowd, and began to hug him.

She began to move backward in awe and amazement. Crawling on her knees, she tried to make no sound, hoping she wouldn't be noticed in the joyous commotion. *The young girl said, "Jesus." It was impossible,* she thought as she added more distance between her and the scene.

Jesus turned around slowly as if he could sense her there. As he turned, Karissa's heart sped up, and she wanted to jump up and run. Instead, she froze. Her heart caught in her throat, and her mouth went dry. When he focused entirely on her, she found she couldn't control the emotions that permeated her body. Her eyes bulged in wide-eyed astonishment. He was the most glorious person she had ever seen.

His hair was like cotton, evenly distributed over his head. His face shone with light that radiated through her soul—he was majestic. His eyes were bright with fire, and he wore a white sash over his chest. It was the purest white she had ever seen. Her eyes swept his body at length as she struggled through her tears. His feet were like burnished bronze and light radiated through him.

He reminded her of the lion she had encountered, and a knowing came over her, and she knew he was the lion. This was Jesus, the great Lion of Judah.

She allowed her eyes to dance in wonder. He stretched His hand out to her. His hands had holes right in the center, though the skin around the holes was healed. Just then, two of the most enormous beings she had ever seen appeared near him. The crowd of people chatted amongst themselves as if they were one big family.

Looking carefully at the beings, Karissa decided they had to be angels. She had a sense of amazement as she took in the sight of them. One had rainbow wings, and the other had wings that appeared to be pearl-like. They had to be ten feet tall with a wingspan of twelve feet wide and hovered over the crowd. She couldn't take her eyes off of them. They seemed to be transparent. She was able to see the group that gathered through their bodies. She heard what had to be hundreds of thousands singing, "Worthy is the lamb that was slain before the foundation of the world."

As the chorus sang, unaccustomed sensations went up her spine and sent chills through her body. She looked around wanting to discover the source of the sound. It seemed to rise within the angelic beings.

The man in white, whom she now knew to be Jesus, stared at her as if there was nothing about her he didn't know. "Karissa, we have been waiting for you," came a sound like the ocean from him. His voice coursed through her and crashed in on parts of her she didn't know existed. She trembled in fear and wonder. Karissa prostrated herself as fear washed over her. But it wasn't like any fear she had ever known. It was more like awe, and it seemed to transform her.

"I am the first and the last, the beginning and the end," Jesus proclaimed. A great wave of wind came from him and swept over her. "Fear not beloved. Before I formed you in the womb, I knew you. You are mine."

Karissa felt unclean. She began to tremble violently. She shut her eyes tightly, sure that she had either gone mad or was in some dream. Or maybe she really was dead. She shook her head in disbelief and tried to remember her life as it was. An overwhelming sense of discontent filled her, and she wasn't sure she had even liked the life she had lived.

Meeting Jesus' eyes yet again, she saw they shone with fire. "Am I dead? I only remember a car accident—did I die?" She dreaded the response because she had so much life on Earth yet unlived. However, she also wished she wouldn't have to leave where she was—with Him.

"No, Karissa, you are not dead in the physical world. Jesus said. Your body is in a coma, but you are still alive in the natural realm." She noticed that He distinctly used the words "physically and naturally" when referring to her death. Did that mean she was dead in another realm?

He seemed to perceive her thoughts and answered them. "I decided that it was time for you and me to meet face to face." He smiled, and it warmed her thoroughly. "Karissa, while your physical body is not dead, your spirit is, and I have come that you may have life and have it more abundantly."

She was amazed, and everything she had ever known, everything she ever was, changed in an instant. And that caused her to have many questions.

CHAPTER 16

Temptation

"Brenda, I'm telling you they shot him right there. It's crazy and I still can't believe it." The words tumbled dramatically from Lucky's mouth.

Brenda sat on the lounge chair shaking as she listened anxiously to all of Lucky's accounts of what happened in The Valley and the streets since she had been in rehab. Her mind was guarded as she listened to her friend's stories up to this point. It wasn't that she didn't care, but she knew if she gave in to her emotions after hearing about the deaths and over doses, she'd want to get high again. If she was honest, she wanted to get high the moment she saw Lucky walk into the visitor's lounge.

Lucky brought back many memories, and she could almost taste the dope in her mouth. But the wind that was in her lungs helping her keep an already wavering guard up was blown into pieces as Lucky recounted Ron's death. She couldn't explain her feelings. Tears pricked her eyes, and she couldn't muster up the strength to wipe them from her burning cheeks.

"Oh, I'm sorry, Brenda," Lucky said pausing to catch her breath. She reached over and gently caressed Brenda's forearm. Lucky felt pity for her friend, but she would be lying if she said she hadn't reveled in hearing the news of Ron's death. All she thought about when the news hit the streets was how he had treated Brenda over the years. Flashes of Brenda's battered body and tears caused Lucky to have no pity on the coward.

Brenda couldn't get the images out of her mind. Ron was set up by two guys who ran drugs for him. Brenda had always known something was up with those guys. She never trusted them since they first started working for Ron.

She remembered the way they looked at her the first time she met them and her skin crawled. One had bucked teeth and lumpy skin, and the other short with the top of his body twice as big as his bottom. Ron was not giving them the money they thought they deserved, and they decided they would set him up and take everything. Little did they know Ron had hidden cameras where the murder took place, and a couple of his partners found the two perpetrators and left their bodies in the same house where Ron was killed.

Brenda felt a great loss no matter how toxic their relationship may have been. She couldn't tell if it was because she loved him or because she knew her chances of easily accessing drugs were over.

She shuttered as Lucky looked at her with pity. But she also knew her friend silently rejoiced that there would be no more beatings and drama where he was concerned. Brenda looked up seeking some form of distraction as she saw people flooding into the lounge. It was Friday, and that's when the patients of Renewed Life Rehabilitation Center got most of their visitors. She scanned the room with a disquieted silence watching tables fill with patients and their loved ones. The music was low but serene, and she loved the lighting in the large, chic room.

She turned her attention back to Lucky who was also taking in the sight of the environment. She must have felt Brenda starring at her because she turned her attention back to her. It was the first time that Brenda paid attention to how her friend looked. Her once even-toned skin was now patchy and textured. She had lost even more weight, and her nails had dirt underneath them. Brenda could tell that Lucky had been having a rough time. "How've you been, Lucky? What's going on with you, and how are your grandparents?"

Lucky smiled sadly, then tried to force a smile. "Don't you go worrying about me," she said trying to joke away the heavy emotions. "I want you to stay on your path and continue getting better. I'll be fine, trust me." Lucky looked down to avoid Brenda's burning eyes. Brenda always had a way of seeing through every wall and defense she put up.

"Grandma Gina passed away last week," Lucky finally said. She paused, obviously fighting for control. She lifted her head back up and met Brenda's stunned and hurt face.

"Oh, Lucky, no..." Brenda got up from her chair and came over to Lucky's side, taking the chair next to her. She pulled the chair close and wrapped her arms around Lucky's frail body. Lucky began to sob uncontrollably, and Brenda looked around, seeing that others were perturbed. She pushed Lucky's frazzled hair to the side, laying her head against her shoulder.

"She was old, Brenda. I know they have to go sometime" Lucky laid her head against Brenda's.

Pulling away, Lucky turned to her. "I've missed you, Brenda. I've been thinking of getting into a similar program like this one and get my life together. It won't be anything this fancy," she chuckled. "Not all of us have well-off family that can move us out the hood." She smiled wryly at Brenda.

"Oh please, they just want me to stop showing up on their doorstep, scaring the neighbors," Brenda teased. She laughed, yet still felt the weight of all Lucky had shared sitting on her like a bag of bricks.

'You know Grandpa Sam is on his last string as well. I don't know what I'm going to do without them. I have to get it together or I know I won't make it." Lucky's eyes dropped to her lap. The smell of smoke and musk from Lucky's hair and body made Brenda nauseous but she refused to show it.

"You know, that sounds like it's the move to make." Brenda turned her head from Lucky as she continued.

"You know I've been going to chapel with one of the janitors here and I've been feeling different lately." She paused and saw that Lucky stiffened. "I thought that God wouldn't want anything to do with me after I screwed my life up so badly and lost my kids." Brenda's eyes stung with tears. And she could feel Lucky's stare as she looked straight ahead.

"I remember when I was younger, I would talk to God all the time about everything. Back when life wasn't so complicated." She broke off into a trance of remembrance. "I thought I had disappointed Him too much, and He wouldn't want me anymore. So, I completely rebelled and tried to shut Him out. But lately, I feel like He's calling me back," she smiled sweetly.

Lucky straightened uncomfortably, pulling away from Brenda. Brenda breathed in heavily, knowing that when Lucky folded her arms as she was doing, she was guarding herself. Brenda had never shared about her lost faith and rebellion against God.

"I'm glad to hear that you are turning to something that makes you happy Brenda. I am."

Brenda knew that her words had some truth in them. She knew that her friend was happy if she was happy, but she also knew that God was not just something that made her happy. But He was indeed the creator of all and wanted to be present in the lives of all. Brenda still battled with feelings of unworthiness and shame, but she was coming to believe more and more that she belonged to Him.

She turned in her seat to look directly at Lucky who absently stared straight ahead. "Look Lucky, you're like a sister to me, and I want to see you happy, that's all. I'm so sorry about Grandma Gina, but she would want to see you doing good, you know?"

Lucky turned towards her hesitantly and exhaled her defenses. "Brenda, don't you think I know that?" Lucky said, defensively. "I'll fight this— I will! I'm tired of this lifestyle too, and I will get it together. Look…" Lucky said as she got up and stretched. "Take care of yourself, and I'll try to come back soon."

When Lucky left, Brenda decided to go back into the lounge to get some coffee and hang out until her Twelve-Step program started in the next hour. Getting her coffee, she sat down to process everything that had just happened. She allowed the warmth from the cup to settle her heart and nerves. So much had happened in the months she'd been away. She knew even if she returned, things would not be the same. *Wow, Lord. I know that you are doing a new thing in me. But my heart is in shambles at all I've just heard from Lucky.* She had grown in her faith a lot over the past few weeks.

Why had she changed so much and so quickly? Two weeks before, she had a dream that shocked her sensibilities. She thought back to that dream or vision, or whatever it was, that she had experienced in her room here at the facility.

It felt as real as the chill she felt from the air seeping through the visitor's lounge window. In the dream she could hear Karissa's voice calling out to her from a large room that was eerily empty. Karissa was a little girl no older than the age she was when she was taken from her. She had her head in her lap, afraid and alone. She tried to run to her, but her feet were cemented to the hardwood floor where she stood. "Karissa, honey, mommy is here," Brenda yelled, holding her arms out so that Karissa would know it was safe to come to her.

When Karissa looked up, Brenda's heart stopped as she saw the most frightened look in her daughter's eyes, and she thought she would die from the pain that wracked her. She fell to her knees and began to weep. When she looked back up, her breath caught in her throat as she saw Karissa was then standing. Only she was not a frightened little girl at all. She was as she must be now—a beautiful young woman. She was radiant, and light shone all around her. She was smiling with a peace that surpassed understanding.

Brenda stood slowly to her feet, stunned and cupping her mouth. Karissa was not alone. There was a man who stood next to her, and she could barely make out his features for the light that radiated from his face. She saw what appeared to be angels standing on either side of them—they were huge and glorious. One angel had wings that resembled the rainbow. *Who was he, the man who stood with her daughter?* She thought to herself but could get no words out of her mouth past the fear.

"I am the first and the last, the Alpha and Omega, the beginning and the end." As He spoke, she saw more angels appear and bow in his presence, singing, "Worthy is the lamb that was slain to receive glory and honor and power." Brenda fell as though dead before him. Although He was a distance away from her, she felt His presence as powerfully as if He was standing right next to her.

"Don't be afraid, Brenda, I am the Christ. Before I formed you in the womb, I knew you." Her body had snapped out of the dream as if something woke her up that was not her own doing. She ran to turn the light on in her small quaint room, afraid that there was someone in the room that she couldn't see. She sat in the middle of her bed with her knees to her chest.

She meditated on what she had seen. She saw Karissa, and she was more lovely than she could have imagined. Why had she seen her first as a child? Was she somewhere hurting because of something that happened to her when she was in foster care or her adopted home?

Guilt gripped her and threatened to crush any form of life she thought she had. But then there was Jesus. Her heart ached with a longing she once had for Him in her youth.

She remembered when she first encountered the presence of God. She was sent to a camp by her grandfather when she was thirteen years old. He hadn't known it was a Christian camp at the time. But Brenda had never experienced anything like it before. She had heard of God and His son Jesus before, but she had never seen people live as followers of Christ. At camp, she saw the camp leaders saying things like, "I'm going to go back to the cabin to spend time with God" and "I'm going to go on a walk with the Lord." She had never heard such talk and yearned to have what they had. She confessed Jesus and was baptized but never told her grandfather, who was Muslim. She was sent to summer camp multiple times until she turned sixteen. But it was hard to live for God when she was home. She felt too weak to resist the temptations that surrounded her.

The day after the dream she went with Frank to chapel for Bible study. When he asked her, as he always did, she told him she would go. He almost looked as shocked as she felt to have moved past her insecurities to accept his offer. That day, Bible study was about how followers of Jesus are invited into a new life when they believe, leaving the "old man" behind. That was something that stuck with Brenda, and she pondered throughout the week about leaving behind all she had ever done and all that she ever was, to cling to Jesus. She thought about how her life could be if she walked once and for all in her new identity in Christ.

The following week, Frank finished his shift and invited her to go to a small group that met every other Friday in the chapel. Brenda again agreed eager to be encouraged again to walk in the new life Christ offered. The group didn't discuss the new life like she wanted them to, but she got something else she hadn't expected. She got to experience people who had battled addictions and shared their testimonies of overcoming by the power of the Holy Spirit. While she still felt her addiction had power over her, she tried with all her might to cling to the freedom they had discovered and were now were living.

All these things flooded Brenda's mind as she sat in the lounge after Lucky's departure. She tried to keep her mind on the positive things that had happened to her and not all the bad news Lucky bore. As she wrestled with her thoughts, Brenda's heart jumped. She noticed something on the floor where Lucky was sitting. Her mouth watered and her eyes danced. She couldn't take her eyes from the object. She meandered over to the chair, afraid, nervous, and curious. Her heart pumped ecstasy through her veins as she scanned the brightly lit room to see if anyone else saw it.

She noticed a couple of young women that she had only spoken to briefly over the past couple of months. The youngest one, Keisha, was engaged in sharing graphic details about a guy she was dating. She noticed others were isolated in their own spaces, watching a movie on the flat-screen television on one of the walls behind her or reading or doing other activities.

Brenda began to tremble as she got up and walked closer to the object. She sat down in the cushioned chair. In a single-minded artful way, she bent down to pick up the object without being noticed. It was a small clear bag with two small white rocks, and all that she had worked for up to this point had left her mind in the blink of an eye. The only thing she could think of was the feelings the contents of the bag would give her. She wondered if Lucky dropped it on purpose or if it had fallen out by mistake. She settled on the latter, choosing to believe her friend wouldn't intentionally sabotage her endeavor to overcome her addiction.

She folded her sweaty fingers around the bag to hide it. She looked around nervously. She slid the small bag into her worn black cardigan. Many conflicting thoughts ran through her mind as she got up quickly from her chair. *Brenda just throw the bag away. This is temptation. You don't want to do this.* Nevertheless, she walked past the trash can.

How was Lucky able to get drugs into the rehab center? The place had security and there were consequences to being caught with drugs—Brenda knew she would for sure be kicked out of the program, shaming Josh and Sheryl yet again.

Her body ached, knowing she was so close to a high as she walked down the wide hallway decorated with modern art.

She wondered where Frank was, and her heart sank at the thought of him. What would he say knowing she had relapsed? Even with great effort, she couldn't stop her growing affection for him. She knew it was best if she pushed thoughts of him out of her mind. Sure, he could relate to her since he also battled a drug addiction, but that was years ago for him. She on the other hand had yet to beat it. She remembered that he frequently told her, "I am just one bad decision away from a relapse. It doesn't matter how long I've been clean. I will always be a recovering addict, Brenda. I'm no better than you or anyone else in here."

Though he spoke with such clear-minded sincerity, Brenda knew that once he found out everything there was to know about her, he would judge her as most did, and rightfully so.

She needed a pipe to smoke the rock, but she wouldn't find one here. *Brenda don't do this— you made it so far, and there has been so much invested this time around,* she tried to reason with herself. She saw some people from her Twelve-Step program walking in her direction, headed for the class.

"Hey Brenda girl, you know we have five minutes before class starts," Deborah said. She looked less frazzled than usual with a little added makeup.

"Yes, I know. Don't wait for me. You guys go ahead. I have something to take care of first." Brenda sped up as she bent the corner, passing a couple of administrative offices. She hoped she wouldn't see Rene.

She was almost to the hallway that led to her room when she heard that steady but firm voice to the left of her coming from the women's restroom. "Brenda, how's it going? You know class is in the other direction?"

Brenda looked away nervously when she saw Rene's careful perusal. "Yes, I just have something to take care of," Brenda said looking away, as was her custom when she was lying.

Rene walked closer, her knowing gaze fixed on her. "Brenda, look at me," Rene said as she stood inches away from her. "This life is what you make it, Brenda. It is what *you* make it," Rene said, eyes deep with understanding.

Brenda looked up at her with disappointment masked in defiance. "I'm not sure what you are talking about. I said that I just have something to take care of before class starts, that's all." Brenda backed away uncomfortably.

"You think I don't see you, Brenda, but I do. I know what it's like to drown in self-pity, guilt, shame, and feelings of unworthiness. But one day I had a decision to make. One day *I* had to choose what legacy I wanted to leave behind for my child. Yes, I screwed up until that point, but how do I want him to remember me? That's what I asked myself. And that answer changed the trajectory of my life." Brenda looked away again with feelings of guilt washing over her. "With all my determination..." Rene continued, "I was completely powerless on my own. But we are never really alone, Brenda. You have all the resources and support to make better decisions."

Brenda stood there seemingly annoyed and uninterested in what Rene was saying, but both she and Rene knew better. "The decision is in your hands, but keep this in mind as you make it...It may be your last opportunity to live the life that you have always wanted to live." With that, Rene nodded her head pointedly at her, and walked away.

Brenda felt she had fallen apart all over again. She couldn't escape the gaping hole in her heart. All the emotions she learned to suppress began to boil to the surface and she thought she would explode. She wanted to escape and desperately needed to because it was all too much to bear.

She started back to her room with great haste, unable to control her emotions. She didn't care what Rene had to say. She may have been an addict in the past but what did she know about her life? She hadn't lost her kids to the system. She didn't lose everything, and she couldn't understand her pain. Brenda thought she could be different, that she could beat the addiction. But then she saw the dope and knew she would forever be a slave. She didn't want to think, didn't want to feel. She began to fidget, looking on the ground, trying to find something to smoke with. She was desperate, and she hated herself for it. All she felt God was doing in her didn't seem to matter when the temptation was before her. *In the world you will have trouble but take heart for I have overcome the world.* The familiar scripture burned in her heart.

Her mind raced, and she decided to head to the ladies' room instead. Most people would be in the Twelve-Step class, or another class or program, for the next couple of hours. Her eyes darted from left to right, and she pushed past the doors that read "Ladies."

"Hey Brenda, good to see you," came a familiar voice. It was Diane. She always tried to avoid her at all costs. Diane was an older white woman who was still getting high but had a way of hiding it. Diane was said to have multiple personality disorder, so you never knew who you would get. A couple of guys said that one minute she was giving them motherly advice, and the very next minute was flashing them and telling them that she knew they had drugs and what she would do if they provided her with some.

Brenda wasn't there to verify it for herself, but she wouldn't have put it past the woman. While most of her encounters with Diane had been positive ones, she had moments where she would see a shift in how Diane spoke to her.

"Hi Diane, how's it going?" Brenda asked unenthused, wanting to continue on her way.

Diane continued washing her hands, snatching the paper towel from the dispenser. She looked at Brenda from the mirror. "My kids are coming up next weekend to visit, and I'm nervous as ever. I don't think I'm ready for them to see me yet. I'm going to clean up, but I just need some time," Diane said, wiping the soft, thin skin under her eyes in an attempt to smooth out the wrinkles.

Brenda stopped in her tracks so she wouldn't seem too inconsiderate. "It will be fine, Diane. Your children love you no matter what." Brenda said, laying a shaking hand on Diane's shoulder. Brenda was unable to take her mind off the bag in her pocket. She was quivering in anticipation. Diane turned around to face her, and Brenda shifted from one foot to the next, trying to maintain her composure.

"What about your children, Brenda? Do you see them often? What do you say to them when they ask you about your addiction?" The questions tumbled out of Diane's mouth brokenly as she continued to wipe the tears before they made their way down her cheeks.

Brenda looked past her to the stall where she was itching to go. "Hey, I'm sorry I have to use the restroom, Diane. But you will be fine—don't stress about it too much."

The smell from the restroom made Brenda nauseous. Clearly, Diane had a lot to release other than tears.

"Ok, I have a class to get to anyway, dear. I will see you later," Diane said and hugged Brenda before she left.

Brenda walked over to the sink and looked at herself in the mirror. Diane's question frazzled her. She looked into the deep brown eyes of her reflection and saw the broken woman that she was. Who was she to think that she could be free from the death grip of her addiction? Her face had gained its fullness back, and the dark circles that had once decorated her eyes were gone. She took the low-hanging ponytail in her hands, removing the hair tie. She combed through her hair with her fingers and put it up into a high bun, so it was not on her neck.

She splashed cool water on her face. She felt feverish. Flashes of her children came to mind as she put her hands in her cardigan pocket and wrapped her fingers around the small bag. She pulled it out and pressed it to her nose, inhaling the scent of it. *Oh God, I thought I was stronger.* She hurried to the furthest stall and pulled the lid down, plopping herself onto it.

She saw two tissue rolls to the left of her. She took the one with the least amount of tissue on it and began to roll the tissue off. Sweat began to bead on her nose. She didn't have a pipe so she would have to make one.

One of the classes she took outside of the Twelve-Step program was about coping with emotions and situations that may be too overwhelming without running to unhealthy outlets. Because this was a Christian rehabilitation center, they brought God into everything. Just then, her thoughts lingered back to the dream that she had and the appearance of Jesus with light all around Him. She shut her eyes firmly trying to block the image out, but she couldn't do it.

She paused, took a deep breath and let it out. She continued unrolling the tissue putting all of her efforts into blocking out any mental images that could distract her. She heard the door squeak open and the wind from the action caused her stall door to fling open. Her heart jumped from her chest as she lifted her foot to shut it. When she heard the stall door open next to her, she rose nervously to lock her door. She was a foolish woman, she thought to herself. How could she not lock the door when she came in?

Brenda sat back down quietly. Putting her face down into her palms, she inhaled silently and exhaled slowly. The quick move to close the door sent a sharp pain from her knee up her leg reminding her that she was no spring chicken, as Sheryl would say. She picked up the toilet paper to finish when she heard the toilet flush and the woman exit.

Thoughts from the dream continued to flash in her mind. She saw Karissa and wondered where the rest of her children were and how they were doing. If she gave in this time, would she ever have the opportunity to be their mom and see her grandchildren one day? Tears rolled down her cheeks and it was all too much for her. *Lord, give me the strength not to do this*. She finished the roll and got up, lifting the toilet seat. She threw the toilet paper in, hoping it wouldn't flood the toilet.

She flushed, watching cautiously when her fear became a reality. The toilet began to flood. She panicked and looked for a plunger. She ran to the other stalls and found one. Running back, she heard the water pouring out onto the tiled floor. Before she could make it back to the stall, she lost her balance and slipped. She tried to grab the stall door to stop the fall, but her knee went out as the full weight of her body came down. She screamed, and the plunger went flying out of her hands. She felt the cool water all up her back and legs. The last thing she remembered before her head hit the floor was the drugs in her pocket.

CHAPTER 17

The Crew

Sariah sat at her desk distracted as she tried to finish a strategy plan for a client. She had been working for what felt like forever to land the account. No matter how challenging life got, she always found joy in helping minority business owners and potential business owners build strong and competitive companies. She loved that she had the privilege to do this and was highly sought after by both startups and established small businesses.

But she was distracted now. She couldn't take her mind off of all that had transpired over the past couple of weeks with Karissa. Looking up, she saw several of her co-workers passing her office through the large open glass doors. Nathalie swung her head in. "Hey girl, you want anything to drink? I'm going to grab something."

"Yes, I'll take green tea, nothing added. Thanks, Nat." Sariah responded warmly, allowing herself to be shaken from her distracting thoughts. She loved Nathalie who was like an older sister to her at this point. She hired her just months after she opened her consulting business. Nathalie was almost ten years older than she was, but she was a fun, energetic person.

She grabbed her phone at the side of her computer, checking to see if Rachel or Brandon texted or called. It didn't matter if anyone else tried to contact her since Karissa's accident. Well, Nate as well. He checked in daily with the rest of them in the chat Rachel created with her, Brandon, and Nate. The four of them had become quite the team. There were many new developments within the last few days.

The day after Karissa went into the hospital, she coded twice. Her heart both contorted within her but rejoiced at the same time. She was sad about the pain Karissa was experiencing but was thrilled the Lord spared Karissa's life. It was a miracle she had survived. The doctors said she had ruptured internal organs, broken her right leg in multiple places, had broken ribs, had lost too much blood, and suffered blunt force trauma to her head.

It was the worst news Sariah had ever received. She called her parents and every believer she knew, asking them to pray that Karissa would wake from the coma and that her life would be spared. By the grace of God, Karissa survived, but that was not the end of their predicament. They had to find Karissa's family because if something was to happen, God forbid, they were not authorized to make decisions on her behalf.

Nate and Rachel were the ones doing the heavy lifting when it came to finding information on her family. At the same time, she and Brandon organized prayer circles and stayed connected on all medical updates. Rachel had worked things out with the hospital, and the medical staff had become fond of them and allowed them to remain by Karissa's side. Sariah even had family members and church family come and form prayer circles around Karissa's bed to pray for her. Karissa's condition was stable as of last night, and that was a breakthrough considering they almost lost her twice.

Nathalie swung back around, carrying a to-go cup in her hand. "Here you go, green tea nothing added." Nathalie smiled pensively, studying Sariah.

"What's on your mind? You don't look too well?"

Sariah rubbed her face with both of her hands before taking the cup. "Thanks, Nat. Just a bit distracted with what's going on with Karissa. Sorry girl." Sariah smiled, willing herself to get it together. But she was in distress with all the new leads that had come of Karissa's family. It never went unnoticed by those around her whenever something weighed on her emotions.

"She's stable now, right?" Nathalie took a seat on the corner of Sariah's desk. Sariah beamed, admiring the easy-going way of her assistant. She was a woman of great faith and had joined Sariah many times in prayer for Karissa's salvation and, recently for her speedy recovery.

"Yes, she's stable," Sariah exhaled, feeling a weight lift off her as she shared. "We have found some leads on Karissa's family, but it's taking a toll on me. I trust the Lord, but I may just need some time away with him in prayer or something," she said, dejected as she sank further into her chair.

"You have been non-stop at the hospital, jumping from one prayer call to the next and looking for Karissa's family. It's understandable if you're a bit fatigued. What new leads did you all find?" Nathalie asked with genuine concern.

She wouldn't have freely shared Karissa's business with just anyone. But she felt Nathalie was a person she could unload on and know it would only go to the Lord in prayer. "Well, Rachel was able to locate Karissa's biological mother, who's currently in a rehabilitation center for drug addiction. Her adopted family is in Gary, Indiana." Sariah pursed her lips.

"Oh wow," Nathalie said, rubbing the back of her neck thoughtfully. "You didn't know anything about her family before this, right? How were you guys able to find out?"

"Karissa never talks about her family or much about her past. But I do know that she was adopted young and that she has not communicated with her family in years." Sariah twisted in her chair as she pondered their discoveries. "Rachel and Nate were able to locate information from Facebook and other sites. I don't know if half the stuff Rachel does to get what she needs is legal, so I don't ask too many questions," Sariah chuckled light-heartedly.

"I don't think they were able to speak to anyone from her adopted side just yet, but they are working on it. They spoke with an aunt or cousin named Sheryl on her biological side, which is how they found out about her mother. No information about her father." Sariah took a sip from her tea and allowed the heat to warm her throat.

Nathalie shifted a bit, letting her hand help balance her on the table. "Dang Sariah, maybe that's why she never liked talking about her past too much. Lord knows the skeletons and grief that may be buried in it. Not just what you all may find, but what may be waiting for her when she comes out of the coma."

Sariah looked knowingly at her. "I know. I've thought about that, and we have all been preparing for it as well." She saw Nathalie wince. "We all know Karissa pretty well. Well, the Karissa of today. Just not much about her past. We know she keeps her past hidden for a reason, but we have to locate someone, because we can't make medical decisions on her behalf."

Sariah paused, taking another sip of her tea. "Looking into Karissa's family will be seen as crossing the line, but I also believe it could be a blessing in disguise for her in the long run." She didn't know if she was trying to reassure Natalie or herself.

"How about you just take the next couple of days off? Andre and I can step up to finish some of the things you've been working on." Nathalie got up and went to Sariah's side, laying a hand of reassurance on her shoulder.

Sariah looked up at her, warmed by the gesture. The smell of her green tea and Nathalie's warm hand sent peace surging through her heart.

"Are you sure, Nat? I can just modify my day a bit so that I'm still able to pull my weight," Sariah said as she picked up her tea. She allowed the heat from the cup to warm her hands before she took another sip.

"Sariah, please. See it as a vacation that you never take. Just show me what you are working on, and let us know what you need from us beyond our current workload." Sariah sighed and knew the Lord was giving her rest.

"It's not a big deal. And I insist," Nathalie said and walked back to the other side of the desk.

Sariah sat up straighter. She pushed her chair back and stood up. Her body tingled from the movement, and she walked over towards Nathalie. "Thank you so much, Nat. It means so much to me," Sariah said tenderly.

Nathalie grabbed her arm gently. "You never ask for anything, so this is the least we can do."

Sariah threw her arms around Nathalie in a heartfelt hug before walking back to her desk. "OK, Nat, I'll wrap up what I'm doing and leave a memo for you on what needs to be done over the next few days. Feel free to contact me if you need anything. I'll still be keyed into my phone."

Sitting back at her desk, she grabbed her phone and sent Amanda a text. "Hey, Amanda! Just an update Karissa is still in the coma but doing better. We have located some of her family members, mostly from the biological side, but still searching for more leads on her adopted mother. Thank you for keeping it all in prayer. I know God brought you into Karissa's life for a reason!"

Sariah finished up what she was doing, wrote up a memo for Nathalie and Andre before heading out.

* * *

Karissa felt pain all over, and she wanted to be out of her misery. She heard noises around her speaking in whispers, and she tried to open her eyes and say something, but she couldn't. Her brain told her hands to move to get someone's attention, but her hands wouldn't obey. She was lying on her back on a bed that felt less comfortable than her own. She tried to will herself to get up.

"Her vitals have been stable, but she is still unresponsive," she thought she heard a baritone voice saying. Her accident came back in flashes. She was texting Steve after running out of the restaurant trying to get away from Nate—*Oh Nate.* The next thing she knew, a big pickup truck was coming at her full speed. Her next memory was being pulled from her SUV with excruciating pain searing through her body.

"Thank you for keeping us in the loop, Dr. Splensburg. We appreciate it," she heard coming from none other than Rachel. Her heart leaped. "Have you seen any signs of movement, doctor?" Her ears had to be playing a trick on her because it couldn't be who she thought it was.

"No, we haven't seen any signs of movements, but we will continue to monitor her throughout the day," the doctor responded. She heard footsteps leave the room and something scraping across the floor—she assumed it was a chair. I'll stay here, Rachel, if you need to go back to work. Sariah should be here shortly."

"OK, yes, I do have to get back. I just wanted to stop in on my lunch break. I can come back after work so that you can go and get some rest. I'll stay until visiting hours end."

Karissa couldn't believe what she was hearing. Her ears had not played a trick on her at all. It was Nate talking with Rachel. And not only that, he, along with Rachel and Sariah, had stayed by her side. She felt a strange emotion that she couldn't quite understand.

A hand wrapped around hers and she knew that it was his. His love for her worked its way across her knuckles and up her arm. His hand was firm yet gentle.

"Sounds like a plan. I'll text the group-chat if anything changes in the meantime." "OK, thanks, Nate." Karissa heard heels clacking across the floor.

"Oh, I was able to get in touch with one of her sisters as well. She said that she would be able to give me a call tomorrow afternoon," Rachel said abruptly.

"Oh, wow, that's good to hear. I'm assuming she's gonna to be able to connect us to their mother, right?" Nate asked hopefully, holding his breath for the response.

"Yes, that's what I'm expecting. We'll see. It's a little funky because technically her adopted mom is the one who raised her, so I'm not sure if it would be her or Brenda who can make medical decisions. But it will be good to get a hold of them both just in case. Sheryl hasn't gotten back to us yet. She's the biological mom's cousin." Rachel sighed heavily.

"Ah, I see. I'm sure it'll all work out," Nate responded.

Karissa couldn't believe what she was hearing. This had to be a bad dream that she couldn't escape. Her heart went from soaring at the thought of the love displayed by three people she loved dearly to feeling as if these same people had just punched her in the gut. They talked about her family as if they had her permission to go snooping through her life. Who did they think they were violating her privacy like this? And how were they able to locate both her biological and adopted family? She fought for understanding through the growing pain of betrayal and embarrassment.

"Doctor Splensburg has been more than helpful, but I'm not sure how much longer he will give us information without a close family member being in the loop," Nate added.

Realizing what was going on hit Karissa like cold water on a sleeper. They had to find someone whom the hospital would deem a relative to make medical decisions on her behalf. She had never shared information about an emergency contact, so someone would have to be contacted who could speak on her behalf. That would have to be a close relative. She chided herself for taking offense with the people who were fighting for her. It was her fault that they had to go through such measures to locate her family. She told each of them bits and pieces about her past, so they must have put all the pieces together to figure out a solution.

She wanted to speak up, but she was unable to talk. She fought for the willpower to move her hand under Nate's to show him that she could hear them, but she couldn't. She began to cry within and wasn't sure if the tears could be seen. As much as she wanted nothing to do with her past, she hated that her friends not only had to look after her but that they were reduced to go into detective mode to find her family.

Why hadn't she made Rachel or Sariah emergency contacts, she thought to herself? Or would that even make a difference in a situation like this? She was tormented by the thought of them finding out about her past, and she almost couldn't bear it. Even though she felt it was inappropriate to be angry with them, she was still ashamed of what they would find.

Nate continued to caress her hand and she didn't think she could love anyone more than she loved him.

CHAPTER 18

The Truth

Karissa felt tired and didn't know how that was possible since she had been lying in a hospital for who knew how long. Flashes of what must have been a dream came back to her conscious and her heart quickened. *Jesus, oh my God, Jesus,* she thought to herself as the memories came flooding in. She heard the monitor's beeping sound and felt Nate tense as he called her name in panic.

All she could think of was Jesus, the Lion of the tribe of Judah whom her soul felt so intimately connected to that she wanted to see him again. She heard footsteps running into the room, screaming from Nate, and someone saying, "She's coding" before she was there again—in paradise with the God-man, Jesus.

She was in complete darkness and she could feel her heart beating out of her chest. She tried to speak and couldn't. Terror gripped her in the pit of her belly. "Oh God, where am I?" she tried to say, but the words wouldn't come. The darkness seemed to have life, and it moved around her—it was loud and cumbersome. Just when she thought the darkness would swallow her alive, a spotlight lit up in front of her and a scene began to play out like a highlight reel.

She saw four children in the backseat of a police car, frightened while an officer drove face forward, unaffected. There was a girl around eight years old with a little boy who looked to be one year old on her lap, crying inconsolably. She saw another boy almost around the same age as the eight-year-old girl and another little girl maybe four or five years old. The younger girl held onto the older girl's arm tightly with her head buried underneath. The older girl holding the child was afraid but had a look of determined strength.

Karissa's heart broke into pieces as she recognized the children. It was the day she and her siblings were taken away from their mother. Just then, she felt a hand touch her right shoulder and a surge of power as if she was electrocuted shot through her. She would have fallen, but the same hand seemed to hold her up. She turned toward the touch, and there He was standing right there looking straight ahead at the same highlight reel.

He looked the same as he did in her last encounter. His face shone brightly, and his skin was a brilliant golden tone.

He had tears in his eyes and her heart twisted within her. "Je-Je-Jesus," and unlike before, her words came stammering out. He turned to her and those same beautiful fiery eyes stared into her soul. She remembered her last encounter with him. She remembered the angels and the throne room. She remembered the beautiful colors she had never seen before, the fragrances she had never smelled before, her senses awakened to a life that was more real than the one she lived before her accident.

She continued starring into the fiery eyes of love standing before her. She was in a trance and the feelings of pure joy washed over her. She felt for the first time in all her life that she was in a place of belonging. She remembered the throne where God the Father was sitting, and she remembered the love she felt from Him. She remembered the Holy Spirit and the sweet communion and connection she felt with Him, and the friendship and grace she felt from Jesus—who was now standing before her.

A sense of unworthiness washed over her. "Karissa, the scene before you is a major moment in your life. Something that was not meant to be broken in you was broken." His words washed over her. She slowly looked back to the scene before her.

The eight-year-old girl, whom she recognized as herself, was stroking the back of her inconsolable baby brother, Caleb, who fidgeted on her lap. One of the officers turned around with a stern look in his eyes and started pointing at the child. She couldn't hear what he was saying, but it was a reprimand. Caleb looked scared and confused as he buried his little head into her chest. The scene continued in a panoramic view, and Karissa could feel herself falling apart inside. "Why…why is this necessary? Why are you showing me this?" She asked in a broken child-like way.

He took her by the hand as the scene changed. She was around the same age walking in a backyard of a bungalow-style house with yellow shutters. The grass was overgrown, and the metal fences were worn down in places. She walked with her head down, running her fingers along the fence. Then her brother, Kendrick, came out from the back door and plopped down on the stairs. It was clear he was depressed about something.

Karissa couldn't hear sounds, but the scene couldn't have been louder. She remembered the moment as if it was yesterday. She and her siblings were at their first foster home with Mr. and Mrs. Caldwell. Living with them had been hell on earth. Jesus gripped her hand, and peace flooded her body. She watched her younger self walk over to Kendrick with concern. His head was in his hands, his shoulders shook and she could see he was crying. Karissa's heart broke for her and Kendrick as she watched the scene. She sat next to Kendrick and wrapped her arms around him, laying her head on his shoulder.

Turning her head from the scene, Karissa fell to her knees and wept. Jesus bent down and touched her head. "Daughter take a look," He whispered. She looked up, eyes blurred with tears, and she tried to focus on the scene before her.

Her heart leaped when she saw angels surrounding them all in the narrow backyard. There was one massive angel with a sword in his hand positioned at the entrance of the yard.

And then there *He* was, sitting on the side of her brother with his arm around him as he cried. She saw herself lay her head on her brother's shoulder, unaware that Jesus was there.

She then saw Jesus reach over to rub her head, smoothing her hair gently. Jesus then laid His hand on top of Kendrick's head as a Father would.

"You were there?" Karissa shifted her position from where she had fallen and bent her knees behind her and faced him.

Jesus bent down until He was face-to-face with her. She studied His mesmerizing features. "I have always been present, Karissa. I have never left you. I have never left Kendrick or Sarah, or Caleb. I will never forsake you."

Through blurred eyes, she saw truth shine through Him, and she believed every word He said.

Karissa felt something that felt like a shimmering wind swirl around them, and it gently swept her face. It felt like a feather and she touched her cheeks, noticing that her tears were gone. She looked stunned and afraid. Jesus chuckled, and it sounded like a river of joy. "Your tears are special here, and everyone that you have ever shed is collected."

Jesus stood up and surveyed His Kingdom with great satisfaction, proud of what He was beholding. "What do you think, Karissa?" He looked at her beaming with questioning eyes. Karissa stood and looked around in wonder. She saw beauty all around. From the stunning mansions, to the streets of gold and the color all around them.

The realization of what shone in His eyes was like a flicker of light to her vulnerable heart. It wasn't that He was just proud of what she was beholding, He was proud that she enjoyed what must have been His very own workmanship. He cared about what she thought as if her pleasure in it is what mattered most to Him. This was all too good to be true. There was no way that this was the One she had run from all her life.

"I'm in complete awe of everything that I've seen, including you. I just can't understand how any of this is real," she said in astonishment.

He began to walk ahead and motioned for her to come along. She followed, taking in all the glorious details of all that stretched out before her. Yet, Karissa still had questions. "If this is so real, then why is there so much pain and suffering in the world? Why did my siblings and I have to go through so much pain? Why don't you intervene with wars and murder?" She tried to remove the bite from her tone.

She stopped walking and noticed that Jesus stopped as well, but He didn't turn around. She was afraid that she'd said too much, and maybe He would condemn her to hell for being foolish. Her heart sank and she lowered her head. "I'm, I'm sorry I just...."

Before she could speak, she felt a hand on the side of her face. She jumped in fear. She hadn't noticed He moved. "My love for you is fixed, Karissa. I can't love you less or more than I do right now, than I did when I went to the cross for you, beloved."

He smiled lovingly at her. "You never need to apologize for sharing your true heart with me. You have and will always be accepted in me." The warmth of His affection filled her, and she fell in love with Him in an instant. He then lifted His hand, and she felt a jarring sensation as He laid it over her eyes.

She was spinning in a scene, and she heard weeping and yelling all around her. She tried to reach for something to stop the movement. "Jesus!" She yelled as the world continued to spin.

Suddenly, she was in a place that looked so primitive it resembled a desert land. Some men looked like Roman soldiers from a book she once read, men and women in ancient clothes moving all around her. She heard loud screams and couldn't believe the scene unfolding before her.

There was a rocky hill with three crosses at the top. On those crosses were men beaten beyond recognition. Her eyes narrowed in on the cross in the middle, and she fell to her face and wept.

All Karissa could hear ringing in her ears was, "I took it all upon myself for you, Karissa, for your siblings, for the world on the cross. I know what it's like to suffer. I have not come to invite you into a pain-free life, but I invite you to live in unspeakable joy with me for all eternity. That's why I shed my blood and suffered on the cross. I want you to be with me where I am."

CHAPTER 19

The Awakening

"Her eyes are moving. Get a doctor," Karissa heard a faint voice say. Feet shuffled at his announcement and noises began to flood the room. She could hear the commotion, a monitor beating in her ears, and someone's hand on her forehead, calling her name.

Her eyes fluttered and sharp pain made her head throb. The light was more than she could handle. "Karissa, do you hear me?" she heard a firm, authoritative voice say from above her. "You are in NYU hospital. You were in a serious car accident. If you can understand me, try to say your full name for me." She heard a male voice that was measuring his words, dragging them out slowly.

She tried to open her eyes again, this time carefully, not allowing too much light in at once. She squinted her eyes but groaned in pain as the light sent a stabbing sensation to the back of her head.

A man in a white medical coat bent over her and Karissa saw Nate behind him, his arms crossed. He began to rub his face roughly, and Karissa could almost feel his anxiety. To the right of him stood Sariah. Her hands were in the praying gesture near her lips, and tears rolled down her cheeks. She felt a hand on her right forearm, and she tried to turn her head, but a sharp pain shot through her neck, down her back, and she gasped.

"Hold still, Karissa. You haven't moved in weeks so you will experience some pain in your neck due to stiffness," the doctor said as he checked her chart and the monitor connected to her body through the IV cords.

"It's me, Karissa. Just relax while he checks you out. You'll be OK," she heard from Rachel and she felt the gentle strokes of her hand on the top of her head. Karissa tried to calm the growing panic that fluttered in her chest. Sariah and Nate drew near with quickened steps and wide eyes. The doctor said something to Nate as he moved back from his examination.

Everything that had happened seemed to engulf Karissa all at once. The confrontation with Nate, leaving Steve at the restaurant, the car accident, the pain from the impact and injuries, knowing that Nate, Sariah and Rachel had been by her side fighting for her, and the thing that struck her most of all...the heavenly encounter.

Was it real? Did I experience heaven, and did I really meet Jesus? She groaned at the ache that throbbed in her right leg.

The dream had felt more real than anything she had ever experienced. Karissa shut her eyes, trying to transport herself back before Jesus. She opened her eyes slowly, but all that was before her was Nate's eyes burning with concern, Sariah's tears, and Rachel's trepidation. She tried to smile as conflicting emotions reeled through her. But she couldn't shake the encounter with Jesus. She now knew He was indeed real. She knew that He had been with her all along. He had shown her things about herself and her past that she had never confronted. She felt she didn't know who she was anymore—or maybe she had never known. She knew one thing for sure. She would never be the same again.

"Karissa, sweetheart, how are you feeling?" Nate asked. He had a firm but gentle hand on her forearm. His touch distracted her from her thoughts. Rachel had come around to the side with Sariah and Nate. Karissa didn't experience pain when turning her head to that side.

"Dr. Splensburg said that your vitals look great and your wounds are healing well," Sariah said with a strained voice. She kept a further distance than Rachel and Nate did, but Karissa knew that she was closer than either of them in her spirit. She knew that Sariah was on her face before the Lord praying unceasingly for her. Karissa tried to lift her hand for Sariah, but even that movement seemed too much. They all caught the gesture and Sariah came forth.

"No 'Rissa, it's fine. I'm here. Try not to move too much." Sariah took her hand.

"You guys have been here the whole time?" Karissa rasped as the tears choked her muffled voice. The small effort hurt her throat. Nate reached over and grabbed a cup of water from the tray by her bed. He held the straw close to her mouth as Sariah reached past him to wipe Karissa's tears.

Sariah's fingers on her cheeks were a cool sensation of reality as Karissa began to fully come to herself.

"Of course, where else would we be? Now you go off scaring us like that again and I'll have to kill you myself." Rachel said as Karissa tried to take a sip of the water. She almost choked on it as the laugh hurt her ribs. "Oops, my bad girl, take it easy," Rachel said jokingly, and they all laughed. The lightness of the moment broke the tension in the room.

It took all of her effort to drag the water from the cup, through the straw, and into her mouth. It seemed even her teeth ached, and her jaw was sore. Some of the water spilled down her chin and into the crevices of her neck. She dragged her tongue across her teeth hoping she hadn't lost any of them.

She was embarrassed and vulnerable, and she wasn't sure how she felt about Nate being there nursing her. The water that did make it in brought her throat and mouth to life.

Sariah worked at cleaning up the water and Rachel pulled up a chair. Nate placed the cup down on the tray and sat in a chair next to Karissa's bed.

"Am I paralyzed?" Karissa's eyebrows shot up, not knowing to whom her question was directed. She glanced at them all as they took seats next to her, with Nate being the closest to the head of the bed. She noticed for the first time that both of her legs were in casts. She felt pain on the right side of her torso and stiffness in the rest of her joints.

"You are so dramatic. You are not paralyzed," Rachel mockingly rolled her eyes. They all laughed this time. "Don't make me laugh. It hurts," Karissa said as she chuckled, wincing at the effort. "No, praises to God you are not paralyzed." Rachel curved her lips in a slight smile.

Karissa noticed the familiar but uncomfortable way Rachel said "God" and wondered what happened with her while she was out. Was Rachel merely saying it not to offend Sariah and Nate or had she come to know the Lord through them?

"You broke both of your legs, have broken ribs, a nearly punctured lung, and head trauma that didn't cause any permanent damage to your brain that they have noticed so far."

Rachel crossed her leg in the chair and Karissa noticed she was dressed in workout gear under her knee-length leather jacket. Had she kept her from being able to work out today? They were all dressed down in comfortable clothes, and she knew it had to be the weekend.

"You coded multiple times, Karissa, well three times including yesterday. It's a miracle you're alive," Sariah said, drawing Karissa's attention back to the matter at hand.

Nate reached over and rubbed Sariah's back. Karissa noticed and felt a sting of jealousy. She hated herself for feeling it, but she did. How close had the two of them become since she had been out? She tried to gain control over her own confusing emotions. She knew Sariah was unequivocally devoted to Brandon, and Nate was clearly still in love with her. But why were her thoughts going down this dark path?

"We took care of some things for you Karissa, so you don't have to worry about anything but getting better," Sariah said as she straightened herself and smiled warmly at her.

Karissa turned her attention to Nate, noting how handsome he looked with his pencil beard and smooth caramel skin. His black polo sweater was rolled up to his elbows making him look chiseled. His body language spoke of self-control and confidence. She felt his protection of her, and it seemed to fill the room.

"You have a long road to recovery, Karissa, but I want you to know that I am here. I will be here," he said as he folded his hands in his lap and stared deeply into her eyes. She knew what he really meant was that she would not be able to push him away as she often had in the past.

"We contacted your company, and they are aware of what's been going on. Your boss and some of your co-workers came by to see you," Sariah said.

Karissa was blown away by how she was cared for—she had never felt more loved. But her defenses went up. While she felt cared for, she also hated it. She didn't like the idea of having to depend on people, and she was not going to allow them to treat her like a child. *Oh, Jesus, I know that you are here. Thank you for my friends, but why am I feeling this way?*

"Guys, I really appreciate everything that you have done, but I don't want you to stop your life because of me. If you fill me in on everything, I can take it from here," she said as her side began to throb. She turned her head up towards the textured white ceiling, not wanting to see the look of confusion and hurt in their eyes.

There was a long silence that lingered in the room. Karissa took a dry swallow, her nerves getting the best of her. She knew that she was not in any position to take care of herself, but she couldn't just sit back and let them be consumed with her problems. She loved them dearly, but she was not about to fall apart in front of them or put her life into their hands. Ironic, she thought, since that's exactly what happened since the accident. She tried to shift a little to gauge her ability and instantly regretted it.

"Karissa, we aren't going anywhere. You would do the same for any one of us," Rachel said, getting up from the chair. She came near the foot of the bed, careful not to hurt Karissa's legs, and took a seat on the edge. Karissa looked down at her with effort.

"I'm not a child, guys, and I don't want you having to change your lives for me. I'll be fine." Karissa looked pleadingly at Rachel and then at Sariah. She was too embarrassed and ashamed to look at Nate as the dark emotions filled her.

"Hey guys, can you give me and Karissa a moment, please?" Sariah said, shifting towards Nate. She placed her hand on his forearm, giving him a pleading look, and then looked at Rachel in the same way.

Karissa burned as she saw the familiar way Sariah touched Nate. She knew the feelings were foreign and that it felt as if they were being placed upon her. *Daughter, these feelings are coming from the evil one. Reject them.* Karissa was stunned. She knew the voice whispering to her soul was Jesus because she recognized the soft and gentle way He had spoken in her dream…or whatever it was. *How could that be?* But she trusted the voice and believed Him.

"Yeah, sure, I actually have a meeting I need to get to, so I'll head out and check in with y'all a little later," Nate said as he sighed, getting up from his chair. Karissa looked at him with a guarded smile as he approached the bed. She reminded herself what she had just heard from the Lord and softened.

"Karissa, I love you and thank God that you are still with us," he said huskily, bending down towards her face. She thought he was going to kiss her and was mortified that he would demonstrate his affection for her so openly in front of her friends.

"I know this is hard for you, but don't push me away," he whispered in her ear. The heat of his breath and the love in his voice melted her. "If you can't see by now, Karissa, my love for you has never died and it never will." He kissed her ear as he straightened, and strolled towards the door.

"Talk to you later," both Sariah and Rachel sang together.

Karissa knew that the three of them had become very close, and the jealousy she felt minutes ago dissipated into shame. She chided herself for her callousness and allowing the *enemy* to deceive her.

"OK, 'Rissa, I will be back later," Rachel making it clear to Karissa that she too would not so easily be pushed away. She hugged Sariah, then bent to kiss Karissa on the cheek before leaving. Sariah looked towards the door, then back at Karissa, before getting up and pacing the room.

"Seems the three of you have become quite the group," Karissa said and tried to shift her body again. "I mean, I'm glad that you guys have. There's no telling where I'd be if y'all hadn't stepped in," Karissa continued, uncomfortable with the silence.

Neither Karissa nor Sariah said a word for a while. Karissa tried to turn her head towards the light coming from the window to her right but groaned in pain at the attempt. Sariah looked towards her with her arms crossed in front of her with alarm.

She walked towards the bed. "Are you OK? Should I get the doctor?" Sariah asked with an attempt at calm.

"No, I'm fine—tried to turn my head again. It's just the way my head was positioned. I'm sure it's nothing serious."

Sariah went to the foot of the bed and stood facing the window, thinking long and hard before speaking. Karissa glanced at her and noticed that she looked tired and worn. She could see unkept hair underneath a pink baseball cap and that she wore an oversized sweatshirt. That look was very unusual for Sariah. Her friend never wore hats. Nevertheless, there was an incorruptible light and grace that shone through her weariness.

Karissa took a deep breath as she grew more uncomfortable with Sariah's presence. It wasn't that she didn't want her closest friend to be there with her. Still, she knew that Sariah wanted to get into her thoughts and determine why she was so insensitive and dismissive to the people who loved her. She knew that if no one could see her true intentions and heart Sariah would.

"You know, the Lord showed me a lot while you were in the coma," Sariah began to move towards the window, never taking her eyes from it. Her moves were slow and calculated. Karissa felt her defenses shaking within her. "I had dreams almost every night, and in my prayer time, the Lord began to speak so clearly to me about you. I even saw things from when you were a child—terrible things," Sariah's voice broke and she put her head down.

Karissa's stomach tightened at her admission and she was speechless. This God she had come to know in her dreams was something else, she thought as she watched Sariah. He must be a mad man to go to such lengths.

Sariah continued, "I saw moments when you were abandoned and all alone," her voice broke off in agony. "I saw moments when you had to protect yourself and your siblings from things that would make the strongest person quiver. I saw a teenage pregnancy and the beating that killed the baby, oh God…." Sariah cried out in anguish as she held herself. "At first I thought I was just having nightmares. But as they continued, I knew God was showing me for a reason." She exhaled a heavy breath.

Karissa couldn't speak past the pain and shock, and she began to shake all over, and tears came streaming down.

"There were unspeakable things that happened to you Karissa, and you have carried it." Sariah walked to the window and placed her hands on the frame using it as support.

"You never muttered a word. You never yelled, you never asked for help, you never said a word." She cried now.

Karissa couldn't escape the emotions that welled within her and she wanted to die. *Oh God, why did you let me live? You should have never brought me back,* she thought as Sariah wept for her. *This is my love poured out for you, Karissa. These are my tears for you that you may know that I weep over you as I sing over you. That you may know that there was never a single moment in your life that I did not see. You were hurt, but I was there, and my strength was made perfect in your weakness.* The voice was so clear that it rang through the depths of her soul, and she was afraid.

"Did you hear that," Karissa asked in a frightful whisper?

"Hear what?" Sariah asked as she dried her tears with the back of her sleeve. She looked concerned and she walked closer to the side of Karissa.

"A voice just spoke to me. You had to have heard it," Karissa said with wide eyes.

A knowing came over Sariah. She stood near the metal rail of Karissa's bed and smiled down at her with fresh tears in her eyes. "There are many ways the Lord speaks to us, Karissa. "There was once a young boy by the name of Samuel, and his story is told in the Bible. He heard an audible voice and thought it was Eli's, the priest with whom he stayed. After hearing the voice three times and confusing it with Eli's voice, Eli finally told him to say, 'Speak Lord, for you servant is listening.'" Karissa looked up in wonder.

"Karissa, the Lord is speaking to you. That should be your response back to Him, 'Speak Lord, for your servant is listening.'" Sariah's heart fluttered at the look in Karissa's eyes. She knew something had softened in Karissa.

"I saw Him Sariah," Karissa said with tears pouring out. "I saw Jesus, I saw God the Father, I saw the Holy Spirit, and I saw heaven. Oh my God Sariah, it was so real and so beautiful," Karissa said, and with great effort moved her hands to her face.

Sariah was shocked and the hairs on her arm rose at Karissa's words. "What! Oh my…" was all Sariah could get out. She could barely speak past the emotions that choked her, and her mouth hung open.

Karissa continued, "He showed me so much, Sariah. He showed me the same moments you were just talking about, and He showed me where He was when certain things were happening to my siblings and me when we were younger. He was right there with me. Like literally," Karissa said with confidence.

Sariah moved to the chair where Nate had sat, closest to the head of the bed. Karissa's eyes followed her, "He was there all along, and He was so real, so glorious. It's crazy—I still can't believe it." Karissa remembered it all as she shared, and her heart flooded with peace. "I don't know what to do with all of it, but I can no longer run from Him," Karissa said with sincerity.

"I have no words Karissa. I keep trying to speak, but I have no words," Sariah said with elation sweeping over her. She hung her head as a soft laugh escaped her lips. *Father, you never cease to amaze me.*

"Wow, Karissa, I can't believe this. Well, I can believe it. You know what I mean," she said as she moved her hand dramatically, and they both laughed through their tears. Sariah thanked God in her heart over and over again. She had prayed for this for so long but had no idea how it would happen. It was above and beyond what she could have ever imagined. "What was it like, Karissa? What happened? How does He look? How do you feel?" spilled out as one long sentence. Karissa saw the hunger in Sariah's eyes and was overjoyed.

Karissa calmed herself and said, "I have so much to tell you, Sariah. But first, I want to accept Jesus as my Lord and savior. Can you walk me through that prayer you told me about before?"

Sariah felt as if she was walking on water and couldn't remember being happier and more amazed. "It would be my absolute pleasure, sis," Sariah said, tightening her lips in a trembling smile. *Oh God, there is no one like you. You are the most magnificent one and I will worship you for the rest of my life and then when I meet you when this life is over.*

Before Sariah could speak, Karissa slowly opened her eyes, allowing more tears to fall. "I'm as bad as you with all this crying" Karissa laughed softly. "Oh, whatever" Sariah laughed with her. "There is so much that I've done wrong, Sariah. I, I…" she stopped and turned her head away in shame. Sariah prayed for guidance.

Karissa swallowed hard and continued, "I haven't told you everything about me. I was afraid," Karissa breathed out slowly. "You know I was pregnant a couple times before?" Karissa forced the question out and agony gripped her. She looked intently into Sariah's eyes as she confessed this and saw no judgment. Only pain and compassion.

"I've given myself to men just to feel accepted. I've manipulated to get my way. I've done so much. I…" she broke, and the sobs racked her body. Sariah placed a hand on her shoulder then smoothed her hair back as one would do to soothe a child.

Sariah tried to speak gently to calm her friend. "Karissa, there are also some things about me that you don't know. I guess I never shared it, because I figured I could just bury it. But the Bible says when we confess our sin, God forgives us of our sin and cleanses us from all unrighteousness. I believe there is power in confessing our pain and past traumas as well." Sariah straightened as she saw Karissa absorb her words.

Sariah told Karissa all about her past and how her father had molested her for years. She shared all that she had dealt with and how hard it had been to forgive him.

Karissa could hardly believe it, and something in her changed towards her closest friend. “Sariah, I would never have known. I’m so sorry. I wish you would have told me,” she said, embracing Sariah with her eyes. She knew it was hypocritical to say since she had kept so much of her past hidden from others, but life became more evident to her. She tried to lift her arms to embrace Sariah. Sariah got up before Karissa hurt herself and bent to hug her.

Sitting back down, Sariah continued. “I hated my father, Karissa. I hated myself. I used to contemplate suicide.” Her voice caught, and she saw the pained way Karissa bit her lip at the admission. “The Bible tells us that all have sinned and fall short of the glory of God. We are redeemed and justified through Christ, Karissa,” Sariah shared passionately. Karissa looked with child-like anticipation into Sariah’s fiery eyes.

“It’s the reason Jesus came in the first place, to save us from the consequences of our sin, which is death.” Sariah noticed Karissa stiffen. “Jesus made a way for us to be made right with God. That’s the good news, sis,” she exclaimed with excitement, and Karissa beamed with hope. “OK,” Karissa smiled, “Let’s pray now.”

Sariah exhaled and her heart swelled. She pulled her phone out, and read Romans chapter ten verses nine and ten from her Bible App, while Karissa soaked it all in.

After repenting of her sins, Karissa asked Jesus to come into her heart to be her Lord and Savior. She wondered what life would be like now. She never guessed that she'd be one of those religious fanatics she always made fun of that hung around Sariah. Would she end up like them? She pondered that question in her heart.

Either way, she wanted to walk with God from here on out. She would have to take it one day at a time. As Sariah welcomed Karissa into the family of God, she shared with her all they had found and discovered about her biological and adopted family while she was in the coma.

CHAPTER 20

The Resolve

Brenda awoke with the most painful headache she had ever had. She winced and looked around trying to figure out where she was. When her vision finally cleared, she recognized she was in her rehab room. The memory of her accident came flooding in, along with a sense of shame with which she was all too familiar.

When she looked to her left, she saw Josh staring at her with ice-cold eyes. She wished she could revert to her unconscious state.

"Josh," Brenda said hoarsely, "where is Sheryl?" She hoped Sheryl was nearby, so she didn't have to face her hot-headed cousin.

"She's working," he answered harshly. He shook his head and placed his face in his hands, clearly upset. "You know what, Brenda, your mother is probably rolling in her grave right now if she could see the way her only child turned out." He sneered with contempt.

Brenda was shocked and hurt. Her pain at his words turned into a hot rage and she swore out loud. "I'm not trying to hear this Josh, so you can leave if you must," she squealed hoarsely.

Josh looked at her in disbelief. He bent forward in his chair, stoned-faced as Brenda continued. "If you're honest, you never cared for me to begin with. But I won't sit here and be scolded by you like I'm a child. You can leave me right here."

"Yeah, that's right, self-pity. That's what you do best, Brenda. Screw your life up and throw yourself a pity party," Josh shot back, sitting back heavily in his chair. "Well, I will not join you in the nonsense. I will not go into every single detail about how I have been there for you even against my better judgment." He glowered at her, and Brenda rolled her eyes, wishing she could escape his harsh but true words.

"How about how I opened my house to you even after you robbed both me and Sheryl blind on your previous visits. How you nearly got me killed when one of your bum suppliers mistook me for someone else when I was coming to bring you a ridiculous care package from Sheryl. Or the numerous times I came to your side after that thug boyfriend of yours beat you half to death. I can go on and on, but I refuse to indulge your senseless accusations. Do you say you aren't a child? Well, it's about time you stop acting like one." Josh could hardly breathe past his anger.

Brenda turned her head from him trying to hide her tears.

"You have no idea what Sheryl and I had to sacrifice to get you into the best rehab center in the region. I hoped you would pull it together this time, but I guess the joke was on me," Josh laughed without humor.

"Before your mother died, she would say you were her pride and joy and said you were going to be special in the world," Josh said brokenly, his voice trailed off in memory.

Brenda couldn't hold her tears back any longer and she turned to face him. He had tears in his eyes. She was stunned as she had never seen her cousin cry before. Her heart ached for him, and she regretted all the pain she caused him over the years. He looked older and weary. *Oh God, I will serve you if you rescue me from this addiction. Help me be who you have called me to be and who my mother thought I would be. Oh God, is it too late for me?* Brenda silently prayed as she felt Josh's sorrow.

"Josh, I'm sorry," Brenda cried out in torment. "I don't want to be this way anymore. I know I have made a mess of my life and God have mercy on me for losing my children. Lord knows where they are," she said and knew deep down that was what hurt Josh most of all. After all, he was the one who tried to help her get her children back when she first lost them.

Josh looked up at her, holding his head high, refusing to give in to his own emotions.

"I was going to smoke those drugs, Josh, I was." she continued to cry. "But I know it was God who stopped it from happening and I believe that He will continue to help me to be clean," she said, pleading with him to believe her. "I have to trust that He can help me, because I can't do it by myself. I can't, Josh." She wiped away her tears again.

Josh shook his head, and an ease came over him. He felt truth in her plea.

He paused as if trying to decide if he should reveal what was weighing on him. Would it propel Brenda out of her addiction, or would it, in some crazy way, drive her deeper into it? He knew the horrible power of addiction, and he pondered the likely result. Finally, he said, "We have located your children, Brenda."

Brenda's head whipped around, and her eyes bulged. "Wha-what?" she said as if a cold bucket of reality came crashing over her. She tried to sit up and groaned at the attempt. Josh quickly came to her side and helped her to adjust the bed so she could move.

"Josh, what did you say to me?" Brenda said, still stunned. She could tell that he was stalling and wondered why he would do such a thing and why he didn't share that information the moment she woke up. She continued to stare at him as if he had two heads.

He sighed and put his attention back on her. He was uneasy. His leg began to shake involuntarily from the stress he was feeling, and that made her more anxious. "Brenda, we were contacted by Kendrick and some of Karissa's friends." He paused and pulled his eyes from her, placing them on his hands which were intertwined tightly on his knees.

"Josh spill it out," she nearly yelled. "Are they OK? Is something wrong with them?" her voice broke into a panic.

"Brenda, calm down. The kids are fine." He exhaled heavily. "Karissa was in a really bad car accident."

"Oh God no…" Brenda screamed. Josh jumped to his feet to her bedside. An alarmed nurse came to the door. "Is everything OK in here? Glad that you are up, Ms. Lyles. Should I call for the doctor?" the concerned young woman asked.

"No, not right now. Just give us a second," Josh said looking back at her grimly.

"Brenda, she was hurt, but she is alive. She will be fine." He uncomfortably tried to soothe her. He always thought his cousin was emotionally unstable at times, and he was uncomfortable playing Sheryl's role.

Brenda had many questions. He pulled his chair closer to the bed and sat down. "It was a miracle they are saying, but we received a call yesterday and they told us she was up after being in a coma and is beginning to walk again. They said she is recovering faster than most would in her situation." Josh rubbed his face roughly. Brenda's eyes flooded with guilt.

"What about Sarah and Caleb? Have you heard anything about them? What about Kendrick? How is he?" Brenda asked holding her breath.

"Yes, we were able to track them down through Kendrick, but we have not contacted them. Kendrick seems to be doing well. I'm sure that once you get yourself together you will want to connect with them. But first, you have to get better. You didn't technically relapse, thank God. They are trying to kick you out of the program since drugs were found on your person, but I'm sure I should be able to work something out with the director." Josh looked at her and took her hand. It was a foreign gesture, but he was trying.

Brenda placed her other hand on top of his, trapping his big muscular hands between hers. "Oh Josh, I will beat this with the help of God, and then I'm going to find my kids and make it right with them," Brenda said determinedly.

Josh was shocked to hear her speaking so candidly about God. He knew she used to talk that way when she was younger. Maybe Sheryl was getting through the snarled barbed wires that had caged her in all these years. "I know you will," Josh said.

Brenda knew two things for sure—she would beat her addiction at all costs and be reconciled with her children. And she would live to share her testimony to all who would be willing to hear. She was convinced that was God's will for her life. She prayed silently that it would be that simple.

CHAPTER 21

The Return

"How've you been feeling this week, Karissa? How has rehabilitation been going?" Dr. Phillips asked through the screen of Karissa's laptop.

After spending weeks in the hospital, she was finally well enough to return to her cozy Brooklyn apartment. Karissa had resumed her counseling sessions once she was able to get around on her own, but had decided to do them virtually until she fully recovered. She was walking pretty well now, but was not one hundred percent healed. "I'm doing a lot better this week. Last week was rough, but that's because I want to get back to normal *like now*," she laughed dryly. "I'm tired of just sitting here like a bump on the log. But I know I can't rush the process," she conceded as she adjusted the computer on her lap. "Ah, rush the process? Way to be self-aware, Karissa. It's good that you noticed that" Amanda smiled as she locked her fingers together on her desk.

Karissa beamed child-like at Dr. Phillips's praise. "Yeah, I know it's been months since the accident, but I still have a way to go," she smirked.

"How has everything else been going with Nate, your mom, and your family? How have you been processing that this week?" Karissa loved the easy way between them and was grateful that she had started her sessions again. If she was honest, she knew she should have never stopped her sessions in the first place. She noticed Dr. Phillips had no bun today and loved the way her silk-pressed shoulder-length hair lay around her face.

"Nate has been wonderful," she blushed. She saw her joy mirrored in Dr. Phillips's face. She sighed, somewhat embarrassed that the mention of his name could cause her heart to respond. "I've given him a hard time, to be honest, but he won't relent." She placed her chin on her knuckles trying to still herself.

"Hmm, I see. Why do you feel you give him a hard time?" Dr. Phillips's face softened, and she sat back in her chair. Karissa looked away and adjusted herself discontentedly. "I don't know. I guess I'm still adjusting to this new life of mine. Everything is different, and I guess it's hard to let my guard down," she smiled somberly.

Dr. Phillips nodded with understanding. "What do you think could be on the other side of you letting your guard down? What do you fear could be the worst that could happen?"

Karissa sighed in an attempt to settle the agitation she felt at the questions. Dr. Phillips rarely gave her answers and usually maneuvered the conversation in a way that allowed Karissa to arrive at the solutions herself. While Karissa saw the benefit in it most times, sometimes she just wanted to know what was wrong with her and save them both the time.

"I guess I don't know what I'm afraid of." The statement came out more aggressively than she wanted. "I'm just afraid, I guess. I'm afraid I'm going to fall apart. I'm afraid of losing control, maybe. I'm afraid of being alone and adrift." She refused the tears that welled. Having to speak of her emotions still caused some anger to arise.

Dr. Phillips smiled coolly, "I understand, Karissa. When we go through so much pain and trauma in our childhoods, especially abandonment by guardians, it's not unusual to fear that others will also reject and abandon us. The fear of rejection and abandonment keeps many from experiencing life to the fullness. It has a way of keeping us away from the very things and people that we love." Dr. Phillips paused, making room for Karissa to respond.

Karissa wiped at the tears before they met her cheeks. She had recently heard about the fear of rejection and abandonment as she faced her past. The first time Dr. Phillips called it out, the words gripped her soul until she felt something lift from within her. She felt lighter ever since. She began to see how some of her behavior patterns aligned with rejection and abandonment. "Yes." she sniffed, "I can see that." Her voice began to soften as her self-understanding began to grow.

* * *

Amanda's heart soared as she saw the way Karissa was responding and the way she was processing her thoughts and emotions. She was pained by the things she had come to learn about Karissa's past and all she had been through. At the same time, she was grateful for how much Karissa had blossomed since their sessions restarted.

She had prayed fervently for Karissa even after she stopped her sessions months ago. She was devastated when she received word from Sariah about Karissa's accident. Still, she sensed the Lord would bring her through it. She felt the need to pray for Karissa unceasingly the entire week before it happened. She had continued in those prayers.

Amanda braced herself for the next question, knowing how Karissa responded during their last session. "Have you thought more about the conversation with your biological mother and doing a session with her?" She held her breath for the response. She saw Karissa's face contort then ease.

She knew Karissa had been working towards forgiveness, but she was still processing her relationship with her mother. A month after her accident, Karissa had spoken with her cousin Josh, whom she had never met. She had shared with

Amanda during a session that Josh wanted her to reconnect with her siblings. He wanted to see if she would be willing to speak with her mother as well. Karissa learned that her mother was doing well in a recovery program for addicts, but it didn't seem to make Karissa more eager to connect with her.

Amanda had suggested to Karissa that she invite Brenda to a session since she was having a hard time communicating her feelings about her mom. Amanda let her know that she would be willing to have a dual session with Karissa and her mom to ease the tension.

Amanda remembered the harsh response from Karissa. Karissa said that being reconnected wouldn't "fix her." She questioned why reconciliation with her biological mother would make any difference at all.

Amanda attempted to defuse that interaction by letting Karissa know it was about the journey, not just the destination. Amanda shared about the potter and the clay mentioned in the Bible. How the clay is not responsible for molding itself, but that the potter was entirely responsible for that. She also shared the scripture in Matthew chapter fifteen about God being the vinedresser and how a branch can't prune itself—it's the Lord who does that.

"I have thought about meeting with my mother." Karissa moved the laptop further away from her face. "I'm down to try it and see how it goes," she said reluctantly and shrugged indifferently.

"Karissa, you don't have to do it if you're not comfortable. It's important that you feel good about it. It doesn't have to be something we rush into," Amanda said.

"No, Dr. Phillips, I think it will be a good thing. I'm a bit nervous and all, but I want to do it. I'll just have to pray and prepare myself. Maybe it's what God wants. It has been coming to mind more often, and I think doing it virtually first may be better for me," she said with a heavy sigh.

Karissa wanted to get it over with if she had to do it to be "healed." She mocked the idea in her head. *Lord, why does it take so much?* Since her surrender to Christ, she felt He sometimes asked too much of her.

"Well, you can continue to pray on it," Amanda said softly. "How about you let me know by the end of the week what you decide?" Amanda knew doing the dual session could be risky but sensed the Lord was pressing it for reasons she didn't fully understand.

* * *

After her Zoom session with Dr. Phillips, Karissa decided to watch a movie and make dinner a bit early. It was a pleasantly warm Saturday afternoon; Nate was out of town and she hadn't made plans for the day. She decided she would stay in and relax.

Turning on a movie she had come to love—*The Shack*—she headed to the kitchen to start dinner. While her injuries were healing well, she still walked with a slight limp and had a soft cast on her right leg, which it gave her problems from time to time.

She allowed the movie to play in the background as she pulled food from the refrigerator. She couldn't help but thank God regarding all that had transpired in the last few months. She laughed. She had even joined Sariah's small group! The truth was, however, she was learning so much—she hardly recognized herself. She felt as if she had been living in a dark cave then stepped into a luscious green field on the sunniest day of the year. She smiled, feeling warm on the inside.

While her relationship with God was growing, things were not so simple when it came to her family. Much had transpired since her friends had reconnected her with them. She discovered that her biological mother was in rehab overcoming her drug addiction. Her biological siblings, Sarah and Caleb, were doing well but were also disconnected from the family. Kendrick had taken to the streets and got into things that tore their family apart in the first place. She sighed and felt sorrowful as she placed her marinated chicken in the oven and started preparing her vegetables.

She was most excited when she reconnected with Sarah two months before. She hadn't seen or spoken to her sister in years. She was more gorgeous than Karissa remembered. She gasped seeing how her sister had grown up when they had FaceTimed.

Sarah had finished college and relocated to Detroit, Michigan, where she worked for an automotive company. Karissa had also made contact with her adopted family. She remembered crying as she spoke with her mother—the one who had taken in her and her siblings. It brought back memories she tried to forget, but the Lord had been helping her to forgive and receive healing. It was painful and made Karissa think of why she ran from it all. But she now wanted to stop running, stop surviving, and actually live for the first time in her life.

Hearing the movie in the background, Karissa allowed the scene of Mack searching for his missing daughter to distract her from her thoughts. She walked to the living room and sat down as her food cooked. The aroma of the seasoned jerk chicken caused her stomach to flutter.

The scene in the movie had always caused her to become emotional. What would it have been like to grow up with a loving father who would search for her with all his heart the way Mack searched for his daughter, Missy? Thinking it over, with her eyes glued to the screen, a knowing came over her and she burst into tears. She had done that a lot since giving her life to Christ.

She knew then that she, in fact, did have a loving father who had searched for her with all His heart. It was Jesus. He had searched for her and pursued her until she surrendered.

The realization stunned her and sent a wave of both grief and joy coursing through her. Grief at her blindness and unwillingness to acknowledge Him. And joy that He deeply loved her more than she loved herself.

She knew then that she would have the meeting with her mother, Brenda. Picking up her phone from the side table, she found Dr. Phillips number, dialed, and left a voice mail. "Dr. Phillips, I would like to move forward with the meeting with my mom. I want the meeting to be in person, though. I will work it out with her and follow up with you. Talk to you soon!" Karissa instantly felt peace wash over her and knew that was the right decision.

CHAPTER 22

Face-to-Face

Brenda arrived in New York City and was overwhelmed by all the busyness and noise. Horns blared, pedestrians yelled on cell phones, and the skyscrapers intimidated her. People moved about in all directions with no sense of order. It seemed chaotic to her. She had never been to New York before and it seemed to live up to everything she had ever heard about it.

She was afraid and felt like a lost puppy. Everyone seemed to know exactly where they were going, but she seemed lost. She preferred to take an Uber instead of the subway. She wanted to get where she was going as soon as possible. She arrived at her hotel and had checked-in with no complications. Now sitting on the loveseat in her room, she couldn't believe where she was and why she was there.

She decided to call Sheryl to pray with her before she went to the therapy session. Closing her eyes before she made the call, she tried to still herself. Her heart beat wildly, and she felt more anxious than she had in a long time. She had connected with all of her kids, but Karissa was the only one to invite her to visit. She loved her children equally but had always felt a special connection with her oldest daughter. She knew there would be a long journey growing in relationship with her children, but this was a start she was grateful to take. *Lord, thank you for this gift. It's more than I could have ever asked or imagined,* she mouthed, allowing the stillness in the room to calm her. She felt the need for a high, but instead picked the phone up and called Sheryl.

"Brenda, how's it going out there? Glad you made it safely."

"Everything's good, Sheryl. I made it here a couple of hours ago and am now just sitting here until it's time for me to go." Brenda slid her shoes off and tried to relax. She was careful not to move too much because she was afraid she would ruin her dress.

"I see, very good. How do you feel about the session?" Sheryl asked, and Brenda could hear the joy in her voice.

"Goodness, Sheryl, my stomach's in knots," she admitted with a slight chuckle.

"I don't know if I can go through with it." Brenda swallowed hard. "I just don't know what to expect." She blew out the heavy air from her lungs as she looked up to the ceiling. "I can't believe I came all the way out here. What if she hears what I have to say and decides she's made a mistake asking me to come?" Brenda stiffened as she felt panic come over her.

"Brenda, it was the Lord who brought you there. He'll walk with you. One step at a time, you'll just have to trust Him. You said yourself it was more than you could have asked for, right?"

"Yeah. That's what I said," Brenda admitted.

"Well, dear, receive what the Lord is doing and go with Him," Sheryl said forthrightly.

Brenda looked upward again, trying to imagine how the meeting would go. "Yeah, I guess that's what I'll have to do. I'm here now," she laughed to take the edge off.

"I can't believe it's happening. But if it will give Karissa the peace she needs to move forward, it will be worth it," Brenda smiled dolefully. "Let's pray, Sheryl, then I'll get ready to meet with Karissa and Dr. Phillips."

Sheryl prayed, and Brenda joined and prayed with all her might. She had never wanted so badly for God to be with her as she did now. She and Sheryl talked a little longer about New York and how different it was from what Brenda was used to in Chicago and Indiana. She hadn't been to many places in her lifetime and felt out of her element.

* * *

Karissa arrived fifteen minutes early at InterFaith Counseling Center. She was so nervous she shook all over. She sat in the waiting room, completely overcome with anticipation.

She hadn't eaten all day and began to feel lightheaded. She prayed with Nate and Sariah moments before she walked in, but it hadn't seemed to still her heart.

She wondered what her mother would look like and if she would be happy to be there. *Girl get it together,* she scolded herself and wiped her sweaty hands on her jeans. She heard the elevator opening and looked up wide-eyed as her mother stepped into the waiting area. Her heart raced and her body felt tingly all over. She saw her fear mirrored in her mother's face.

She looked very different from the last time Karissa saw her. She wore a coral dress that flowed at her calves and black kitten heels with an open back. Her hair was pulled back in a ponytail. Her mother's shape was similar to her own, but her mother was a little shorter. Karissa noticed her mother's eyes immediately welled with tears when she saw her.

Karissa stood suddenly and clenched her hands at her side. Her heart beat wildly in her chest and she felt a little lightheaded. Her mother walked slowly in her direction, and Karissa took a few steps towards her. "Ma," she said brokenly as they stood face to face.

Reaching towards Karissa's face as if she was a vision, Brenda's lip trembled. She pulled Karissa into her arms powerfully and held her tight. Brenda began to weep, and Karissa felt the regret in her mother's strong embrace.

Pulling back and holding her daughter at arm's length she smiled through her tears, "You are gorgeous, Karissa." She pulled her back into an embrace and kissed her face. Karissa felt like a little girl in her mother's arms. She allowed the fragrance of her to course through her senses. She tried to imagine that she had spent her entire life with her mother as she was in this moment—sober, strong, and focused on loving her.

Pulling away, Karissa studied her mother's face as emotions welled within her. She felt a little under-dressed in her jeans, blacktop and flat slide-ins. "Thank you," she said, blushing and looking over her shoulders, hoping Dr. Phillips would come immediately. "I'm glad you made it," Karissa said uneasily as she guided her mother back towards the chairs.

Before they could sit down, Dr. Phillips called out their names. "Ah, Karissa," she said brightly. Karissa turned and felt relief that she wouldn't have to sit with her mother alone. "And you must be Brenda," Dr. Phillips smiled kindly. "Please come back."

* * *

Brenda felt her senses whirling as she sat in the office. The smell was pleasant, and everything looked expensive. She loved the evergreen plants and the brightness of the room. She felt insecure and wondered how much her daughter was paying this woman to fix problems she had caused.

She smoothed her dress, wondering if she looked OK. Sheryl had bought the dress for her since she wanted to make a good impression. She knew her daughter would not be ignorant of her financial condition, but she wanted Karissa to see that she was not the same woman she used to be.

When Dr. Phillips spoke to them both about the session beforehand, she told them she would not charge for it. Still, if they wanted to continue doing sessions together, she would work something out with them.

Brenda couldn't stop starring at her daughter. She looked like her father but had Brenda's smile and body build. Her hair was fuller than Brenda's, and she could tell her daughter was doing well for herself. She wanted to weep as she looked at her. She didn't want to make her uncomfortable, but she wanted to hold her and never let her go. She could tell her daughter was a lot stronger than she was. She smiled inwardly at the fact. She had prayed her children would be stronger than she had been. She could tell Karissa tried to suppress her true emotions, and that broke Brenda's heart.

"I'm glad you decided to come, Brenda," Dr. Phillips's calm voice broke her uneasiness and caused her to relax a little. She could see Karissa was trying to relax as well.

Brenda tried to speak past the shakiness in her voice. "The flight wasn't bad at all," she said as she looked down and placed one leg over the other. "It's pretty busy here compared to Indiana and even Chicago. So many people. But I'm fine," she laughed nervously.

Karissa didn't laugh, but looked at her with a forced smile. She adjusted herself in the recliner to see her clearer, and it reassured Brenda that she did want to be there.

"That's good to hear," Dr. Phillips said as one side of her mouth curved.

"Yeah, it is," Karissa added, clearly having a hard time engaging. Brenda noticed that Dr. Phillips recognized it as well and looked intently in Karissa's direction before continuing.

"Brenda, as I mentioned when we spoke, I have been seeing Karissa for a while now. I am walking with her through this part of her journey," Dr. Phillips turned and smiled tenderly at Karissa. "And prayerfully beyond, I hope."

Brenda could see the therapist was fond of her daughter. Would Karissa have needed the attention of a therapist if she had been the mother she needed? She pushed the self-condemning question down and prayed silently that God would help her avoid being distracted by her guilt and shame. She was there for Karissa.

"I believe having you two come together in this setting will not just help Karissa step further into the healing process, but it will be the door for the two of you to step into the relationship I know you both desire to have with one another." Dr. Phillip sat back in her chair and opened her notepad.

Brenda stared longingly at Karissa. Her daughter remained silent and Brenda wanted to know what was going through her mind. "Thank you, Dr. Phillips. I would like that very much. Whatever I can do to help Karissa get whatever she needs, I'll do it." Brenda's voice broke as she looked at her daughter.

Karissa looked over and felt uneasy that the focus was so much on her. She noticed the selflessness in her mother's words and softened. She saw the tears in her mother's eyes for what they were—feelings of unworthiness and guilt. She wanted to say something but couldn't. She was grateful when Dr. Phillips broke the silence.

* * *

"OK, if you two don't mind, I would like to pray over our time, and then we can jump right in." Amanda prayed. She saw that both Brenda and Karissa relaxed more and the tension in the room calmed. She was grateful that the sun peered through, brightening up the dark emotions laying beneath the surface. Amanda's heart ached for them, and she believed they would experience a breakthrough before they left her office—she had prayed fervently for it.

She couldn't help but think of how Brenda must have turned a lot of heads back in the day. She admired the beautiful smile and deep dimples. She wondered how much more captivating Brenda's smile would be when she decided to forgive herself.

Amanda looked intently at them. "I want to say that this session is to help give the momentum needed to start building wholeness both individually and collectively. Not just for the two of you but also the rest of your family."

"Yes," Karissa responded simply, unsure of what to expect.

"How about we start by sharing what you hope to get from our time today?" Amanda gestured with both hands, signaling that either of them could start.

Karissa started, "I have questions." She looked at her mom and Amanda saw the vulnerability and accusation in them. "I don't know what I want the result to be, but I guess I want to understand how things happened the way they did. Like how did you end up losing us?" Karissa sighed and seemed to release her inhibitions. Brenda pursed her lips and exhaled deeply as she looked at her daughter with pained regret.

"And you, Brenda?" Amanda asked with a tone of earnestness. Brenda swallowed and looked in her direction. "I know I have messed up so much with my children." Her face twisted in anguish. "I just want to get it right with them and if they and the Lord allow it, I want to be in their lives." She paused, looking at Karissa. "I would like to be there for my daughter now if she will allow me." Tears wet Brenda's cheek. Amanda motioned for the tissue box next to her chair, and Brenda bent to grab it. Karissa gave a strained smile at her mom.

"Karissa, you said you had questions you wanted answered. Would you like to ask your mother those questions now?" Karissa crossed her legs and looked from Amanda to her mother. She exhaled and turned in the recliner to face her mother.

"Yes. Ma, what happened?" Karissa asked. She sniffed and her lip trembled. "Why did you leave us?" This time the tears came. Amanda could tell Brenda wanted to get up and embrace her daughter but restrained herself. Instead, she reached out her hand in Karissa's direction and drew it back shakily. Amanda watched and prayed silently for them both.

It was a while before Brenda could speak. "I was so lost, Karissa. And I was not strong like you are." She choked back tears and continued. Brenda looked off with suffering eyes as if the words were too much to bear. Karissa looked at Amanda and fidgeted in her seat. Amanda nodded in Brenda's direction, encouraging Karissa to engage in the moment.

"I felt so alone, and I got caught up with the wrong people." Brenda looked back at Karissa with pleading eyes. "I never intended to get hooked on drugs and I never ever thought I'd lose you or your brothers and sister." She looked at Amanda as if the statement was not just for Karissa but for her as well. "I left you all in the shelter because I was so depressed. I thought I'd lose my mind."

Karissa dapped at the corner of her eyes and sat straight-backed while her mother continued.

"I just needed to get one high—that's what I told myself. Then I would be back," she wept.

"Take your time." Amanda's soft response broke the tension. "One high turned into another, and before I knew it, days had passed." Brenda reached down grabbing another tissue and blew her nose. "I'm sorry," she said, feeling shame for the decisions she had made.

Karissa said nothing for a long while. Amanda wasn't sure if she would speak. Then she softly answered, "It's fine, ma," Karissa said, and Amanda could see she meant it. She noticed compassion in Karissa's demeanor for the first time since they entered the office. She knew that Brenda's honesty was doing more than she may have known.

Brenda went on to tell her daughter about the day leading up to their separation. By the time she made it back to the shelter, she learned that Child Protective Service had taken them. She said she was raped by a taxi driver and left for dead on the side of the road before she could get to the shelter. After finding her children were gone, she attempted suicide. She said her life went into a downward spiral, knowing her kids would be put into a foster home unless she could prove she could take care of them.

"I felt so empty inside and I had no idea how to pull myself out of the pit I was in. The thoughts that have tormented me most was that I knew my kids were better off without me." She then got up from her chair and went to Karissa. She slowly bent before her and placed her hands on her daughter's arms looking straight into her eyes. "I'm more sorry than I'll ever be able to express, Karissa. I didn't deserve you or Sarah, or Kendrick and Caleb. But you'll always be the best thing that has ever happened to me."

Karissa turned, covering her eyes with her hand. Amanda's eyes welled up, and her heart twisted. She prayed to help keep her focus on the mission at hand.

Brenda continued to pour her heart out to Karissa.

"Don't ever think for a moment that I didn't want you and that I didn't love you. I thought about you every day," she rubbed Karissa's shaking arm. "Every birthday, I thought of what you would look like, who your friends would be," she sniffed. "I thought about if you had boyfriends and if they were good to you. I imagined it, and I kept the images with me all the time as if they were a lifeline. I've never stopped loving my children. Not ever, Karissa."

Karissa turned her head back to her mother and allowed the walls to come down. She threw her arms around her mother's neck.

"I thought about you all the time," Karissa said, weeping.

Brenda pulled her closer and drew her head down on her shoulder. Brenda looked over at Amanda, who was dabbing her own tears. Amanda knew the session had come to an end in the best possible way.

Amanda knew this was not the end of the journey, it was just the beginning. Karissa knew that as well.

CPSIA information can be obtained
at www.ICGtesting.com
Printed in the USA
JSHW020752010621
15393JS00001B/6

9 780578 916149